ECLECTICA

Absent-Minded Art

Volume one

A colouring book by
Stuart Royce

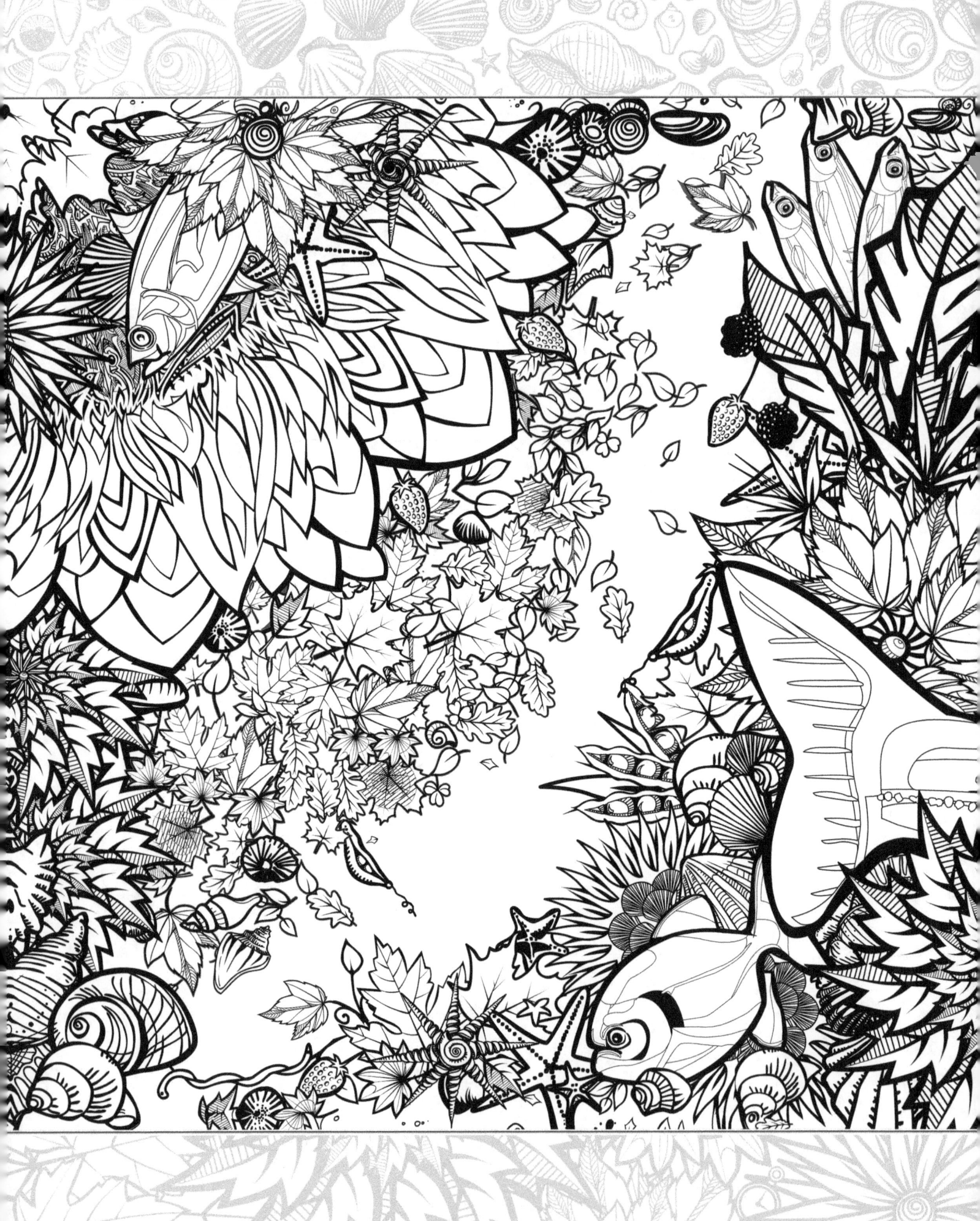

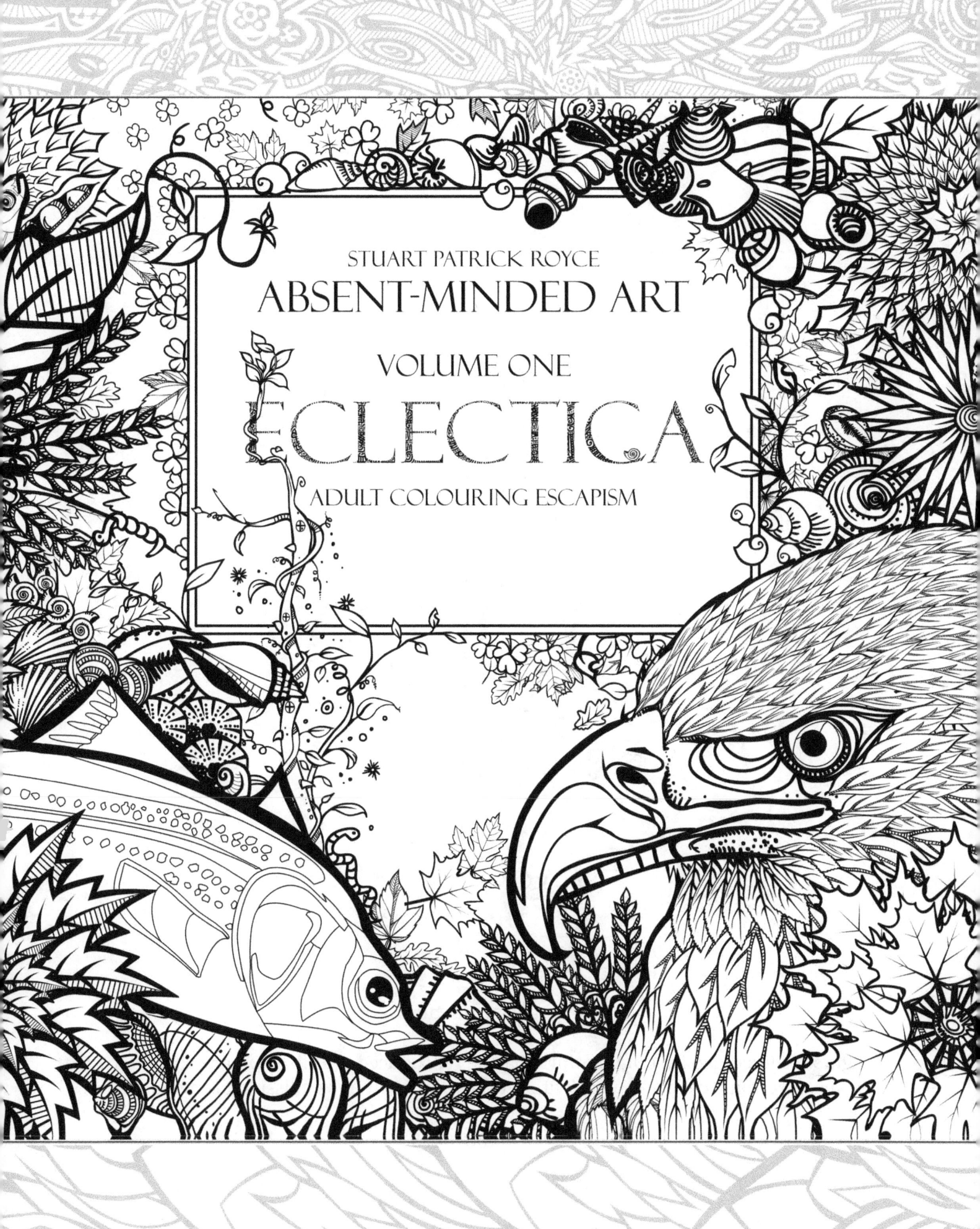

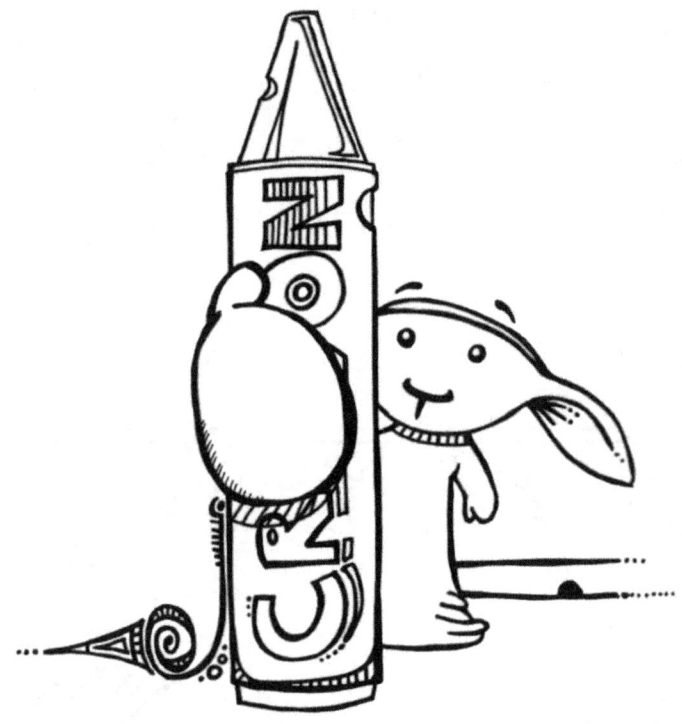

NO, LAMMIE...
YOU'RE GOING TO NEED
MORE THAN CRAYONS!

ISBN-10: **1532895305**

ISBN-13: **978-1532895302**

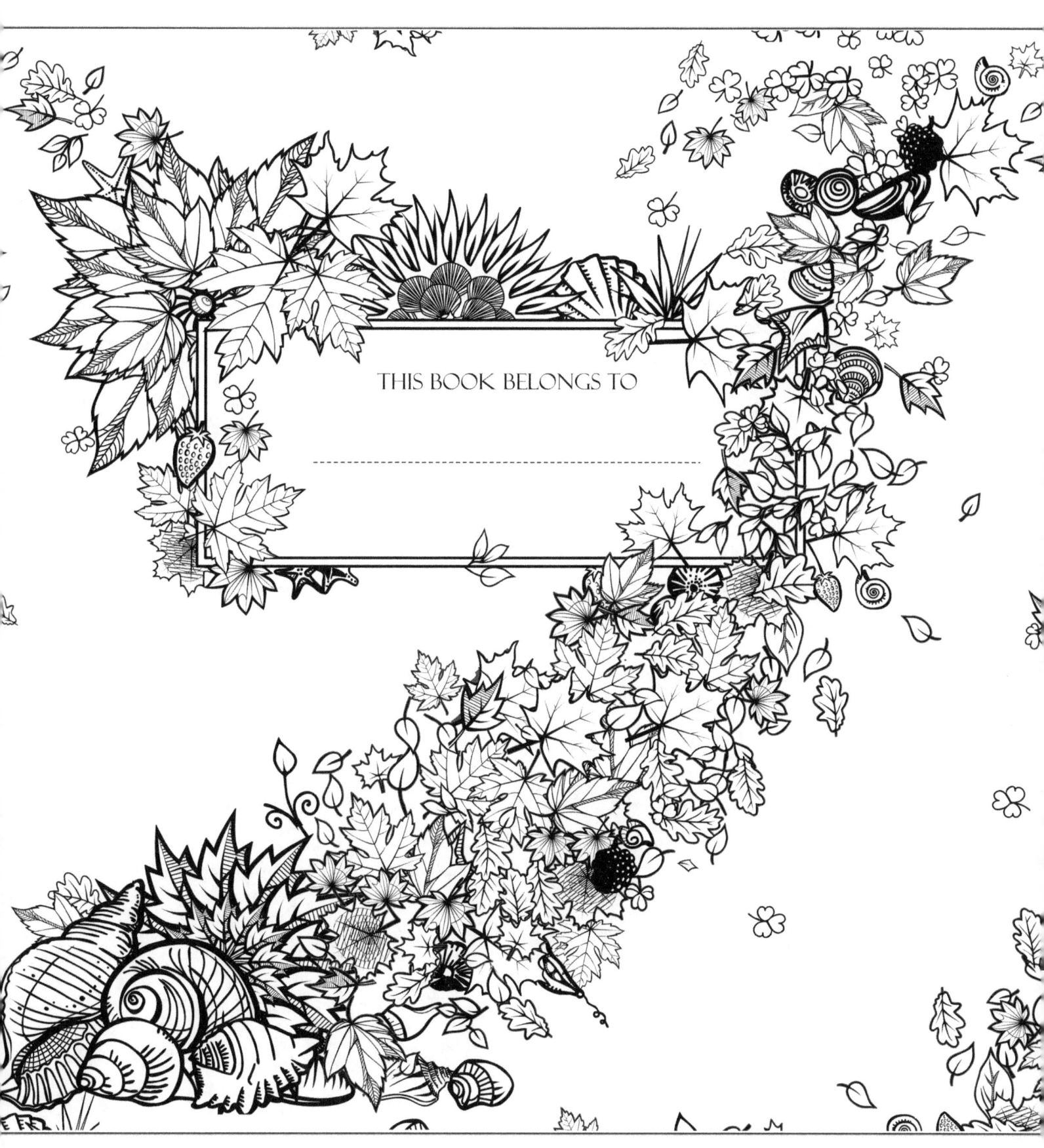

THIS BOOK BELONGS TO

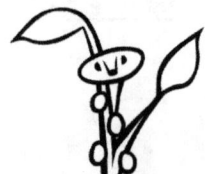

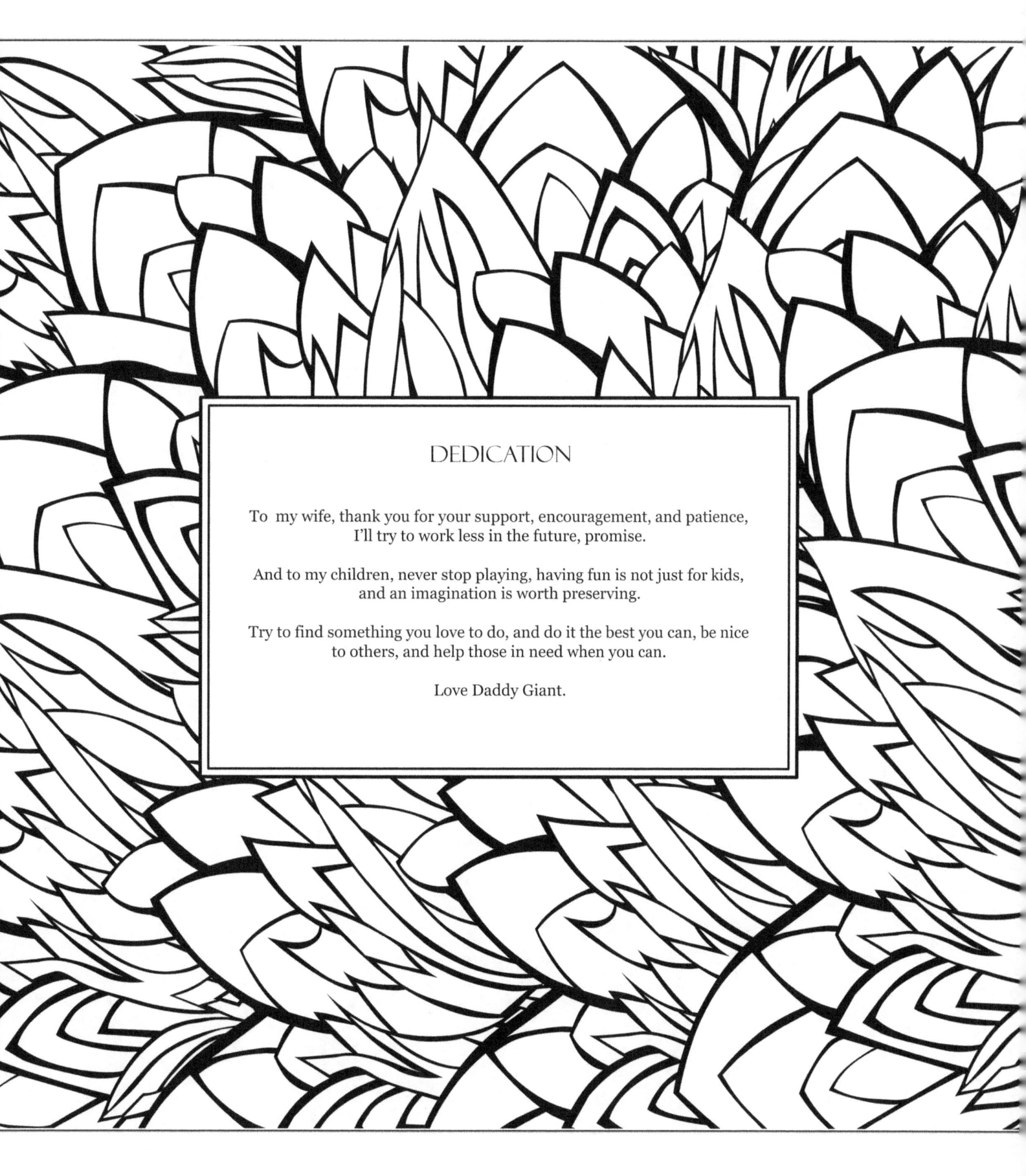

DEDICATION

To my wife, thank you for your support, encouragement, and patience,
I'll try to work less in the future, promise.

And to my children, never stop playing, having fun is not just for kids,
and an imagination is worth preserving.

Try to find something you love to do, and do it the best you can, be nice
to others, and help those in need when you can.

Love Daddy Giant.

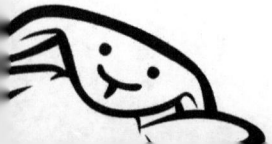

CONTENTS

This colouring book has over 50 creations
for you to lose yourself in, from the
zen-like repeat patterns and intricately
detailed abstractions to chaotic double-
page spreads, they will all take a steady hand
and an adventurous mind.

Several of the designs have also been
duplicated and given an extra dimension of
complexity -not only to give you more to
colour- but also to provide you with a
challenge and encourage you to look again,
but from a different perspective.

Why not get started with this little
gem to the right?

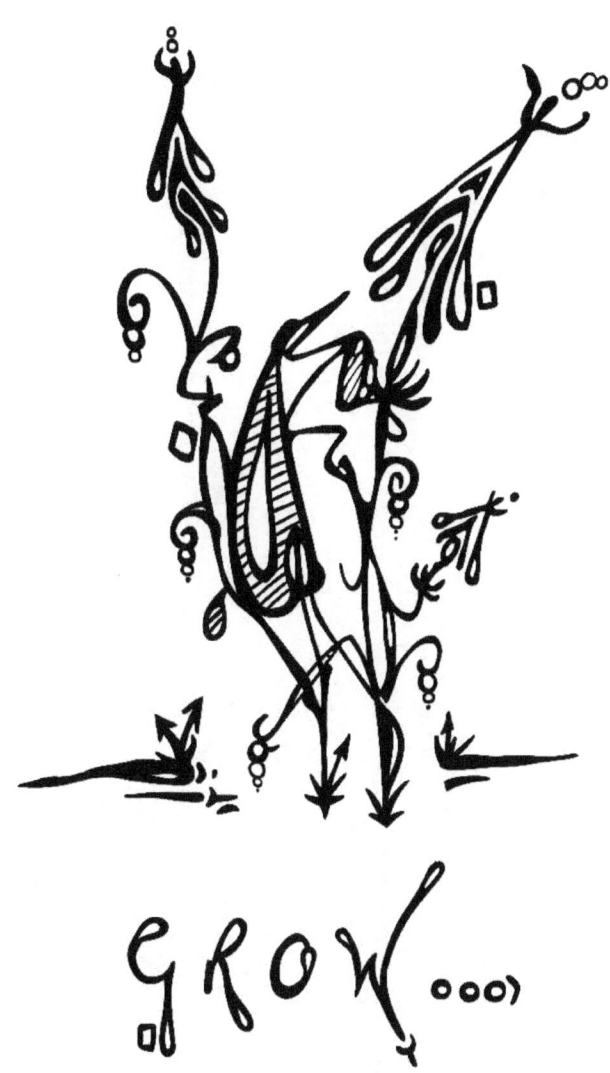

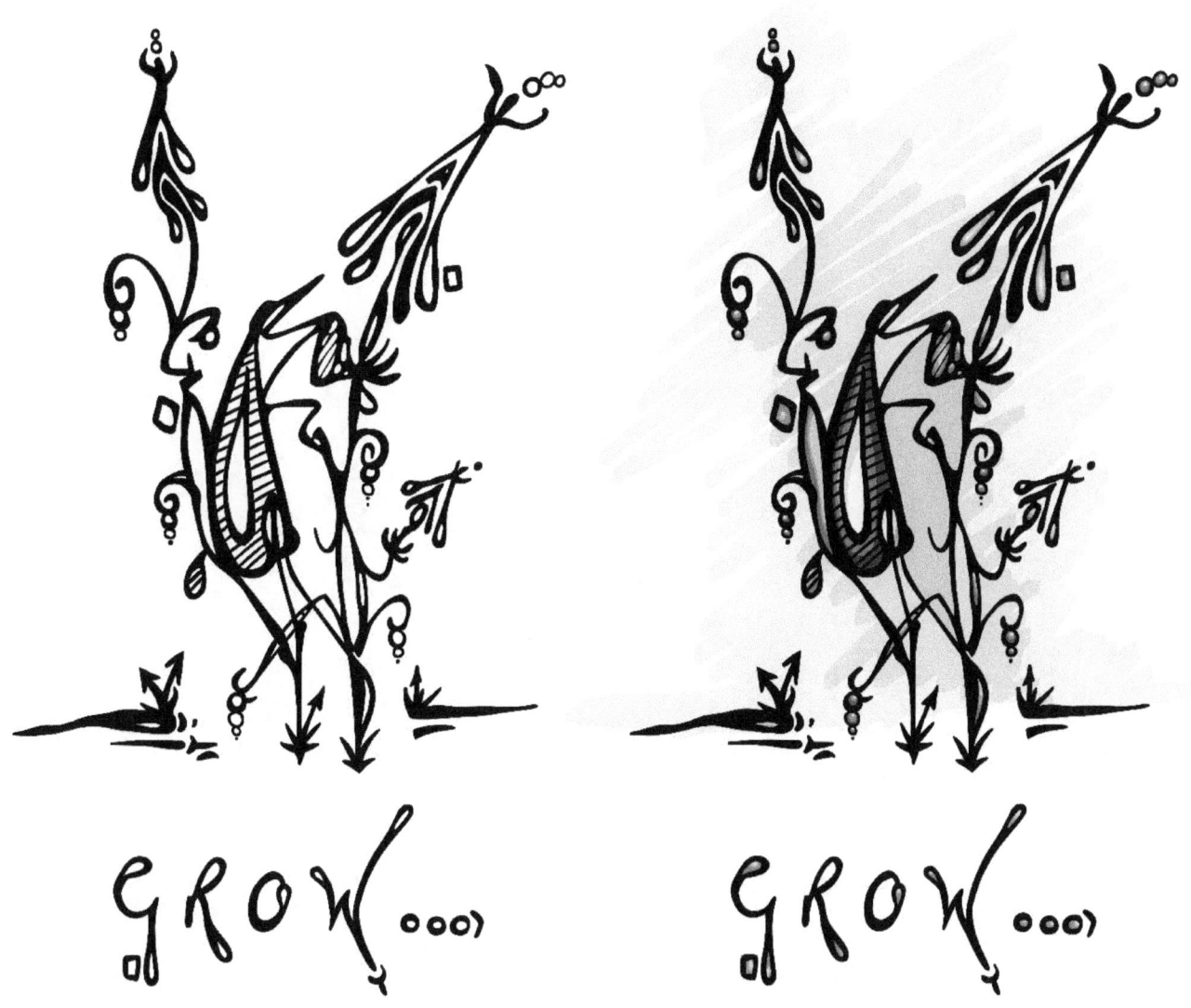

GROW....)   GROW....)

To view these in colour visit https://www.facebook.com/StuartRoyceArt
You can also pop over to www.stuartroyce.com to find out more.

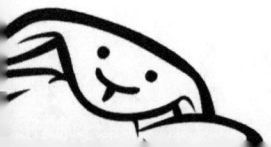

I'd really love to see the artwork that you make with this colouringbook and anything else you create too
Share with me and I'll share it with my corner of the world

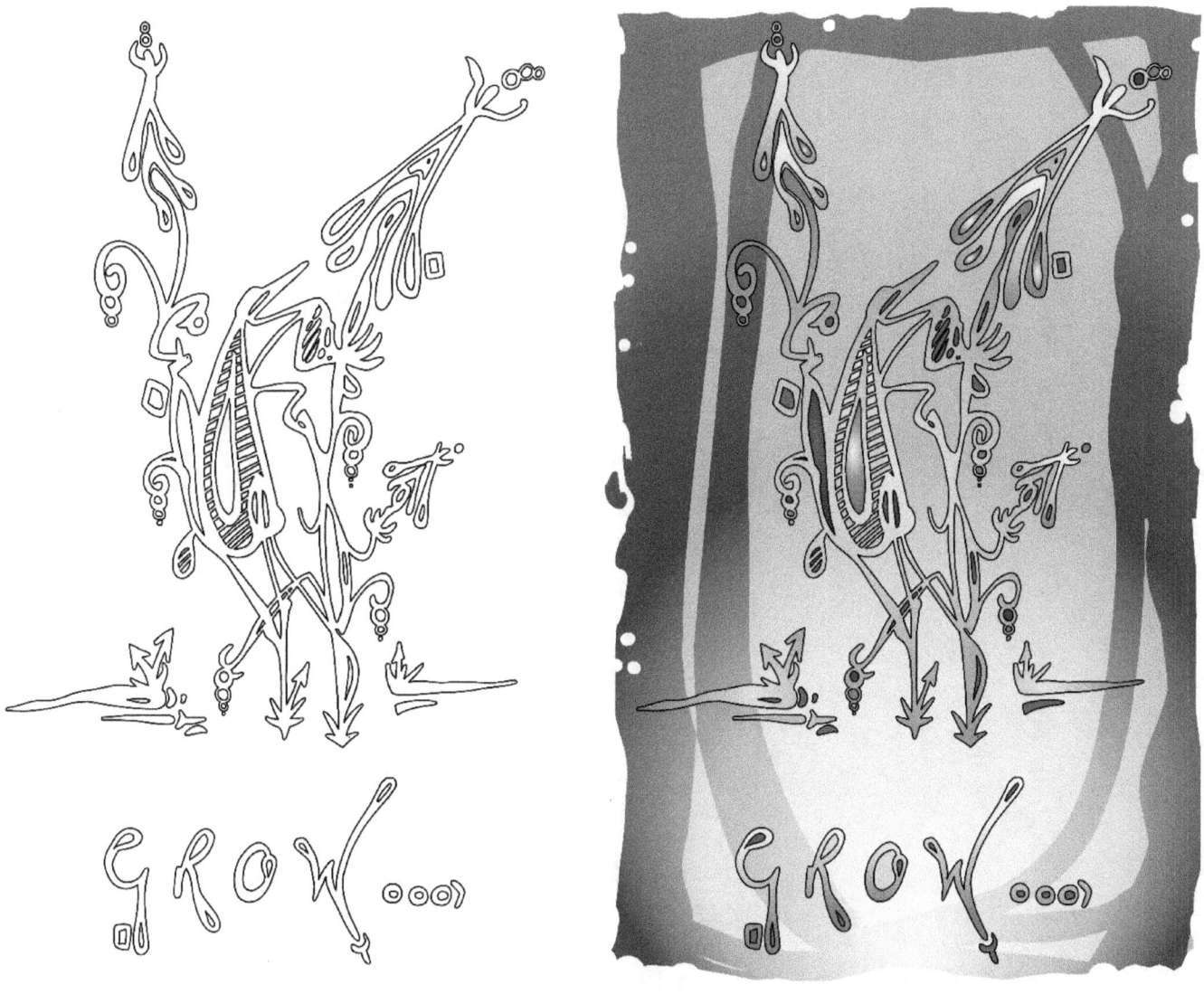

https://twitter.com/StuartRoyce

https://www.facebook.com/StuartRoyceArt

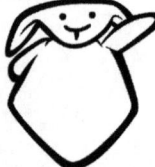

INSTRUCTIONS

For some additional fun, here are some collectibles to look out for.

I sprinkled these three in for my daughter as they're her favourite things, how many of each can you find?

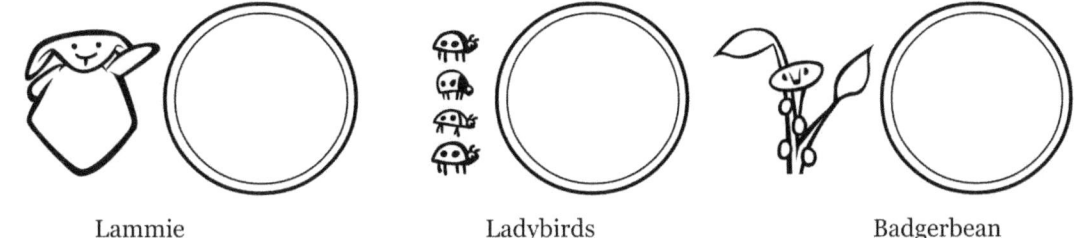

Lammie   Ladybirds   Badgerbean

There are one of each of these little doodles, can you find them all? Tick the boxes when you find them.

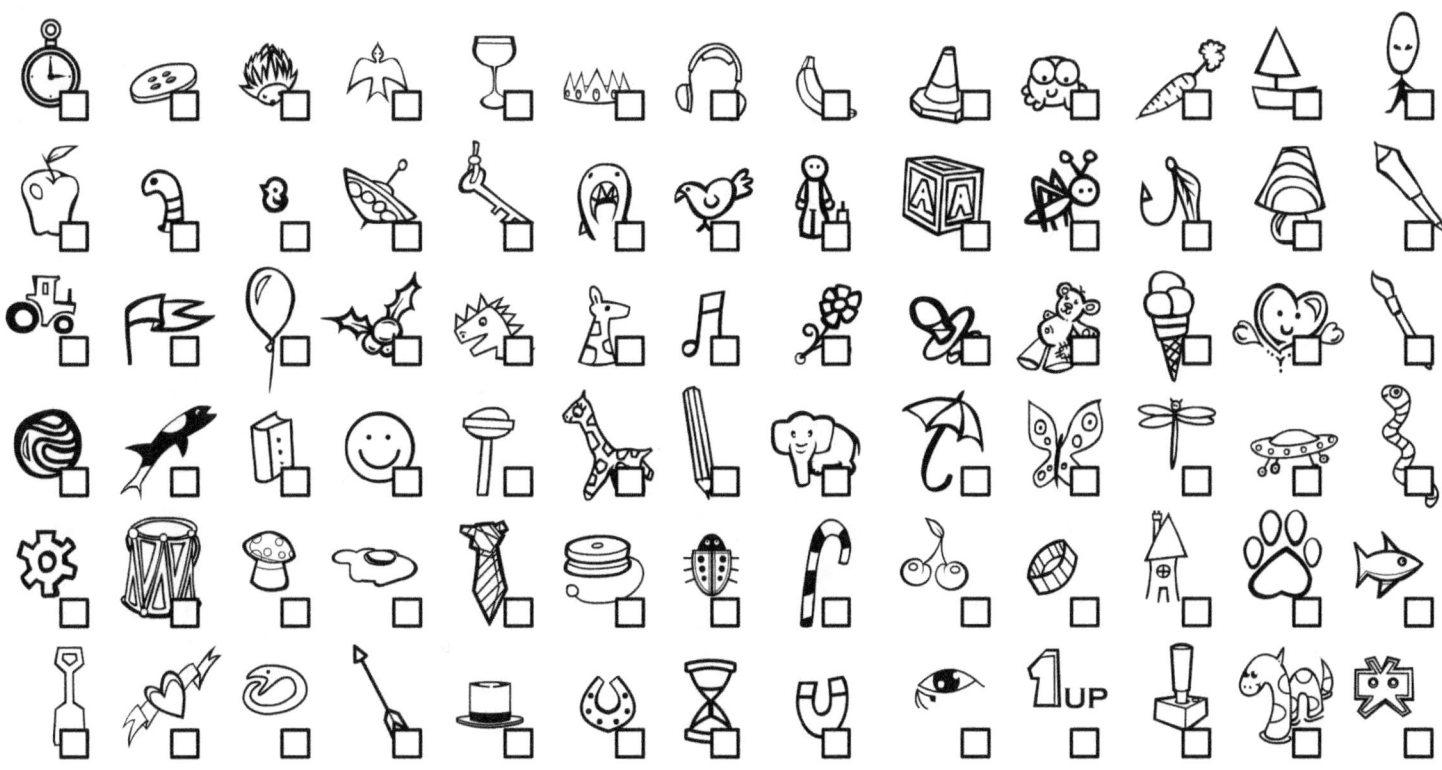

PART ONE

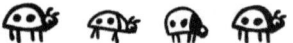 A FASCINATION WITH SHELLS >>

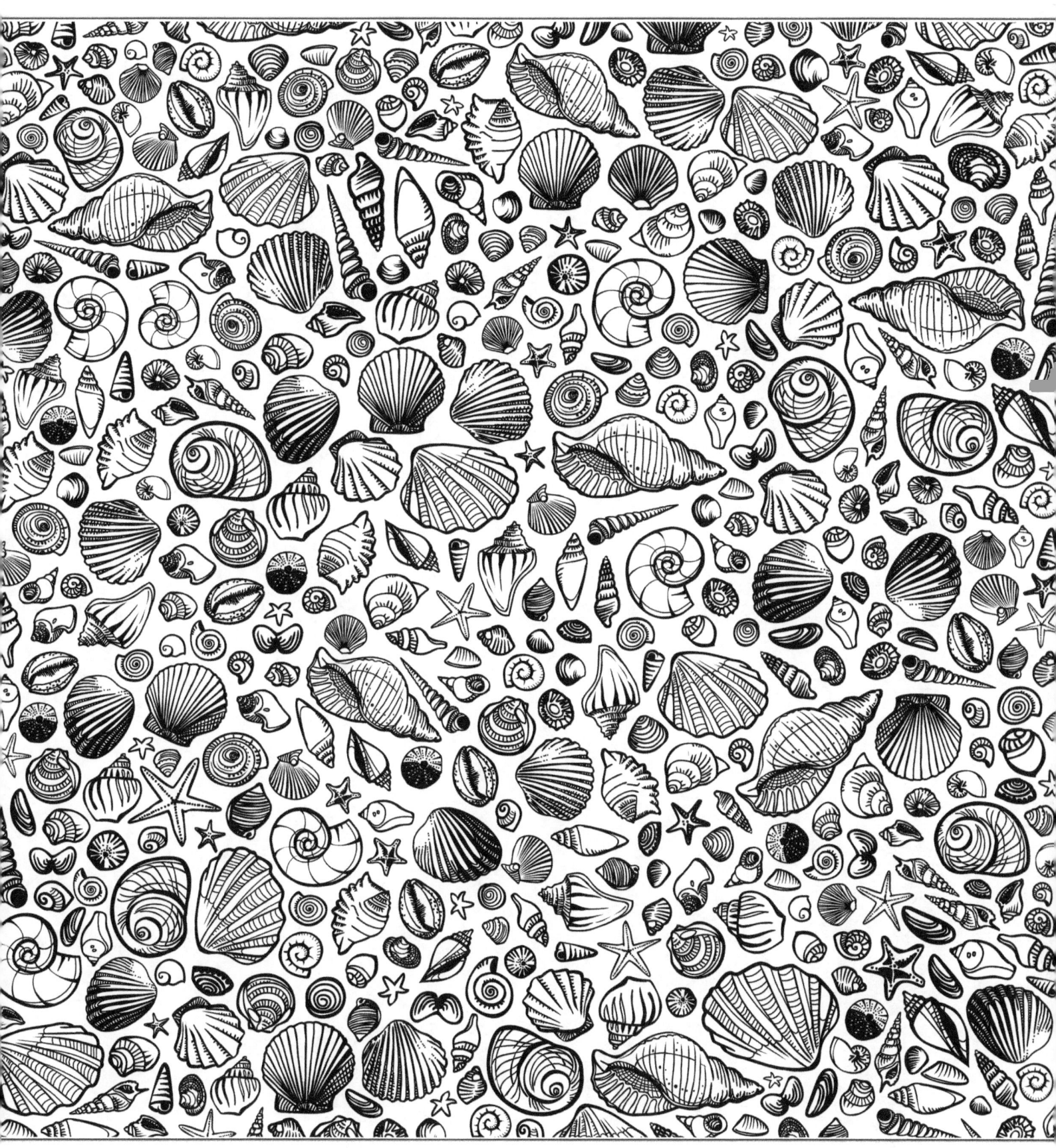

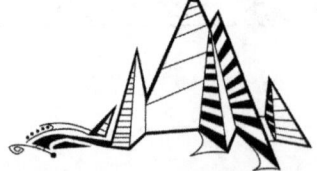

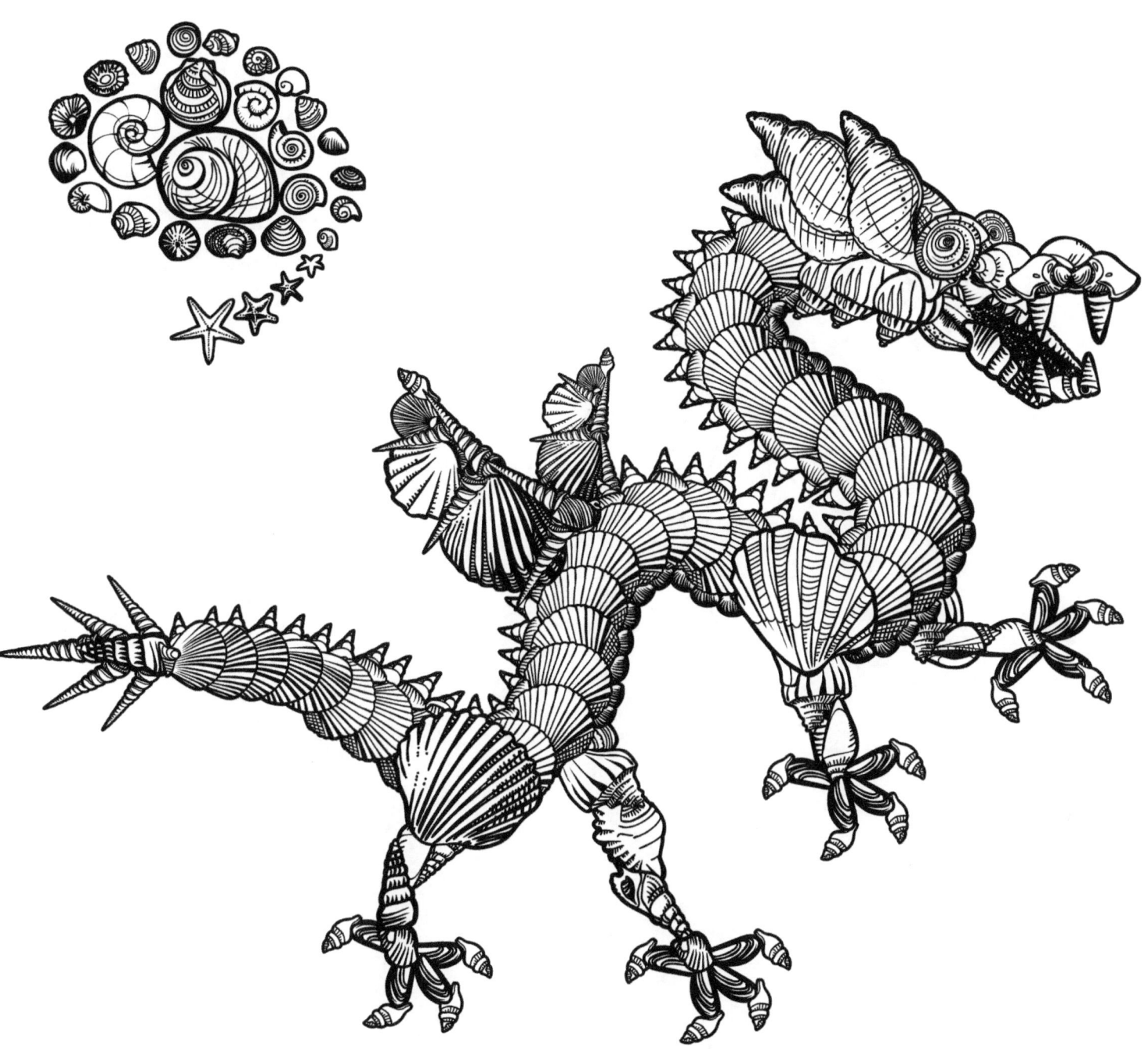

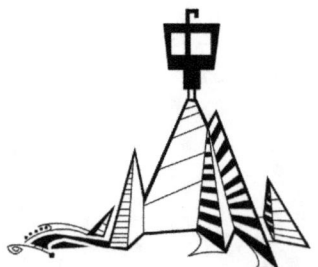

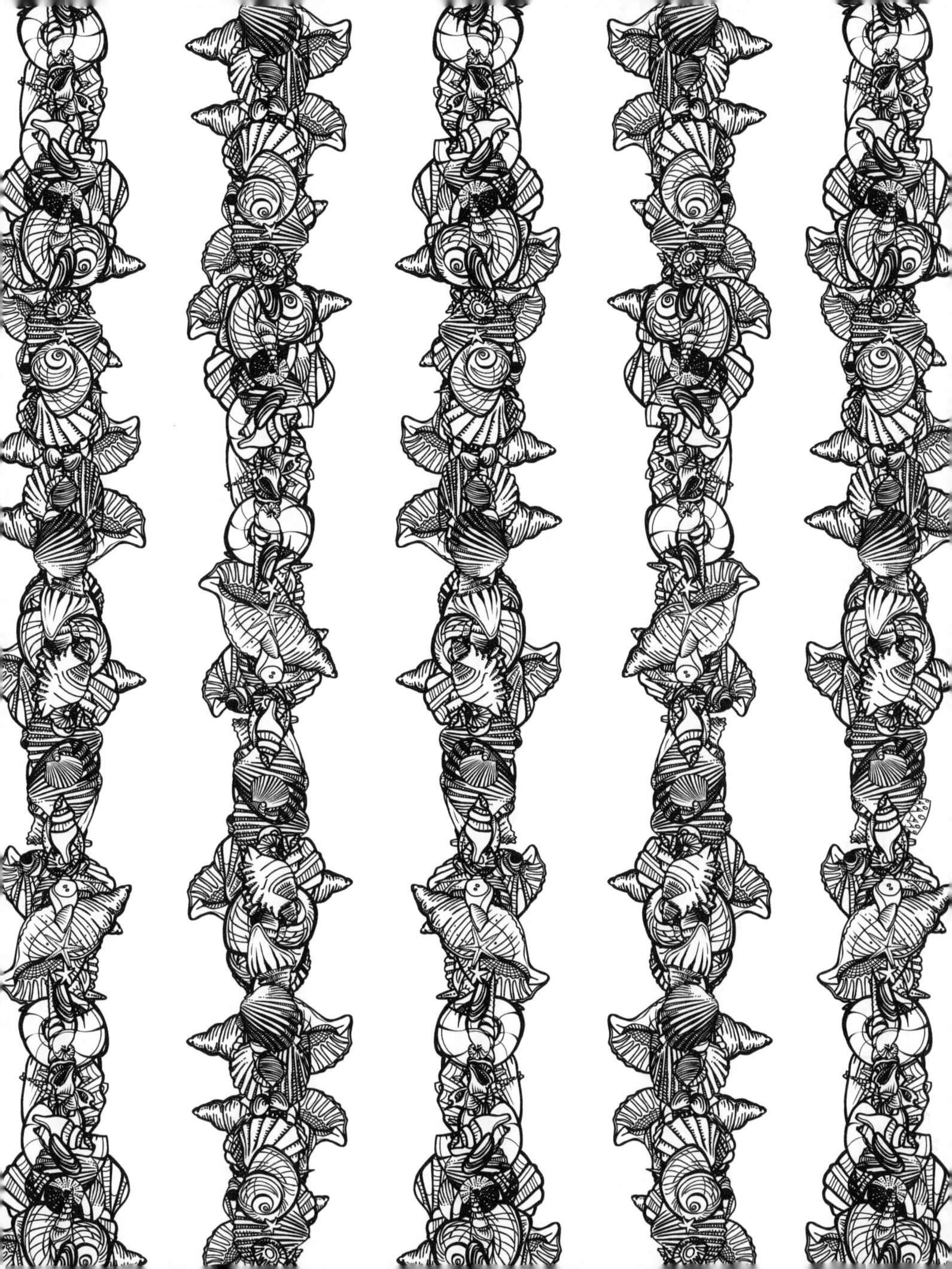

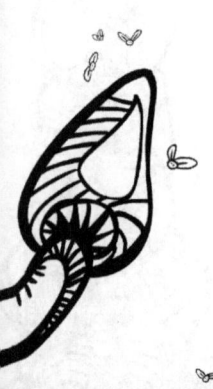

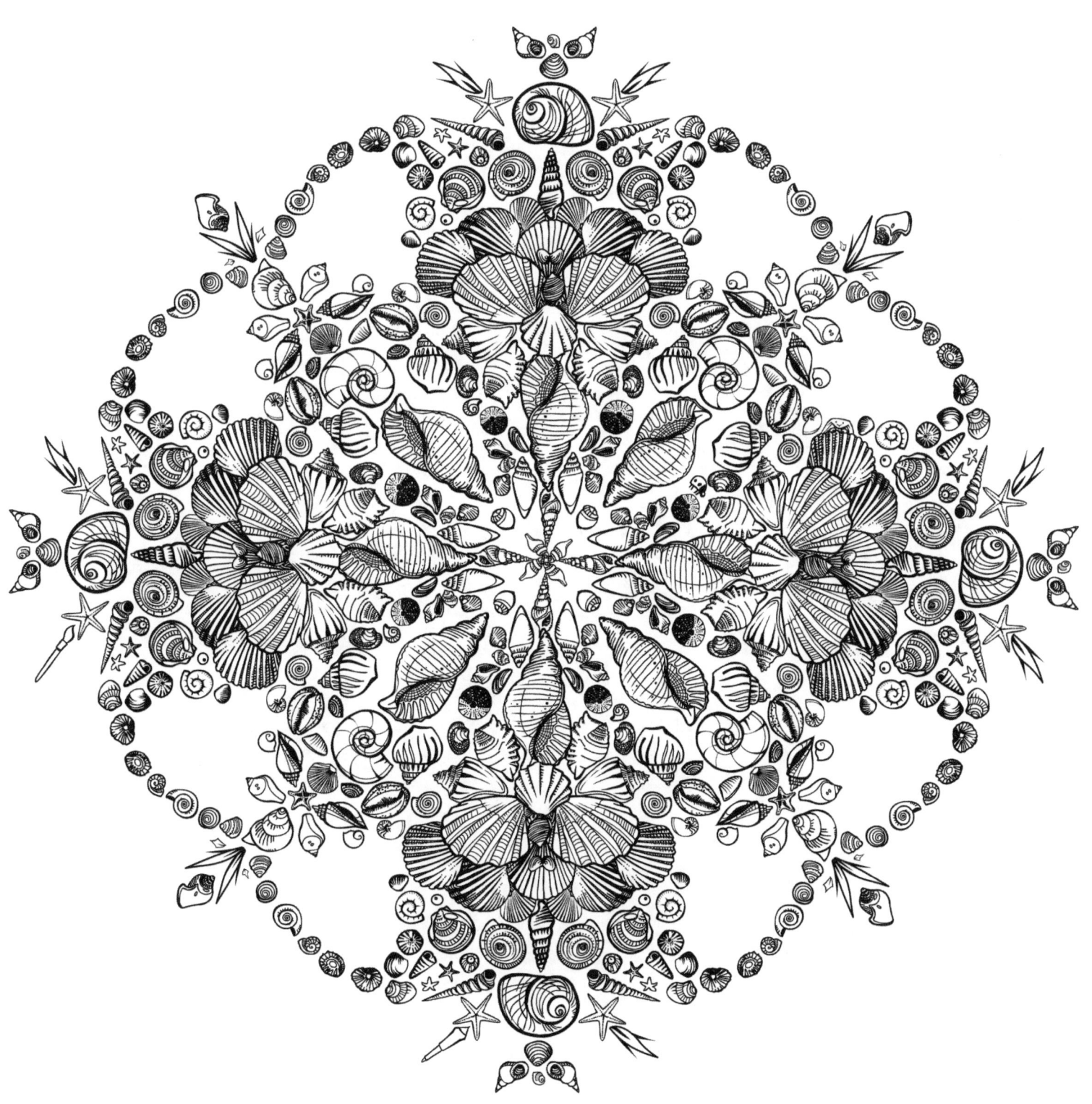

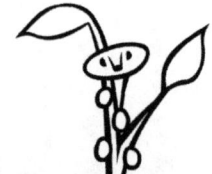

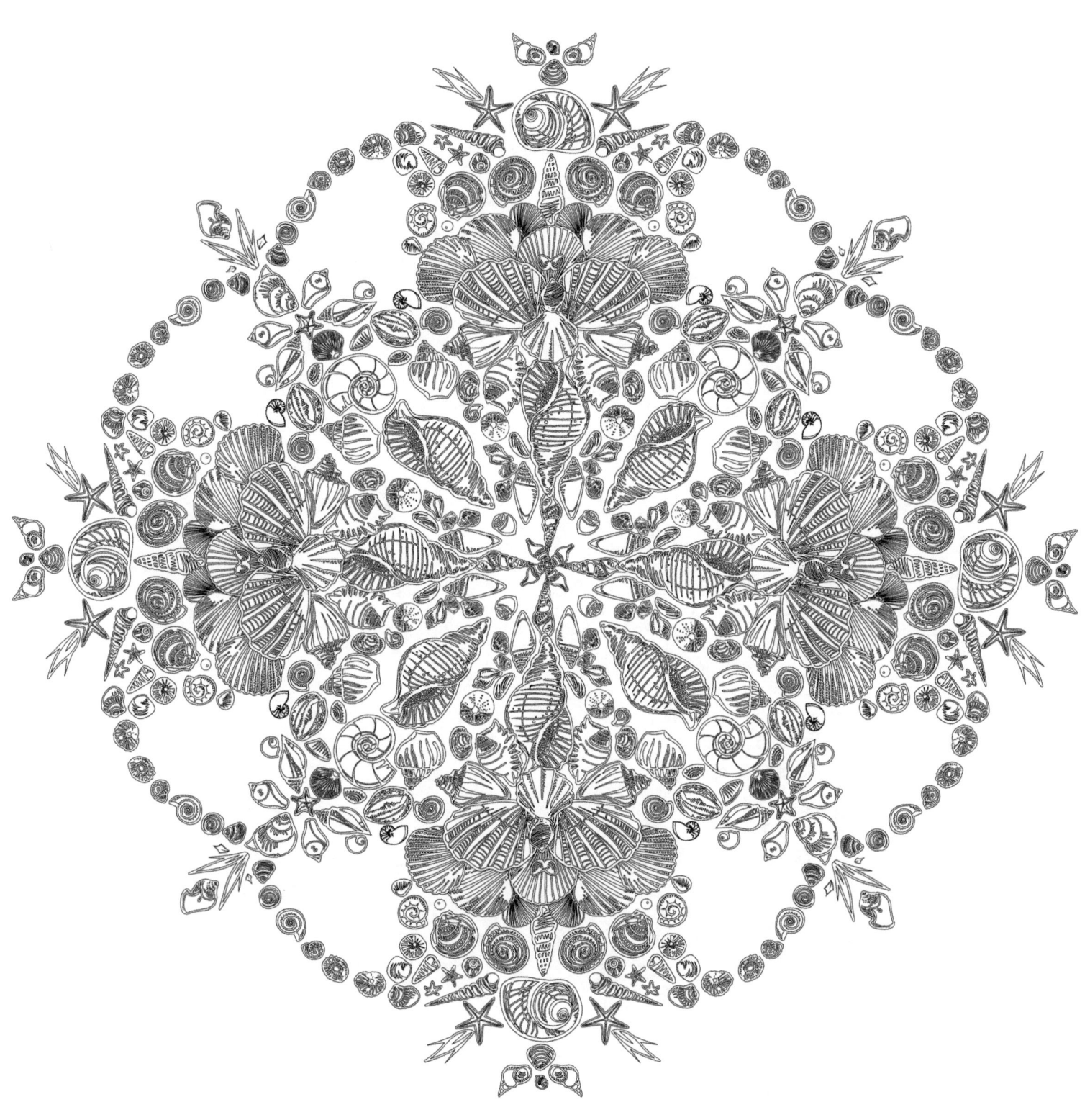

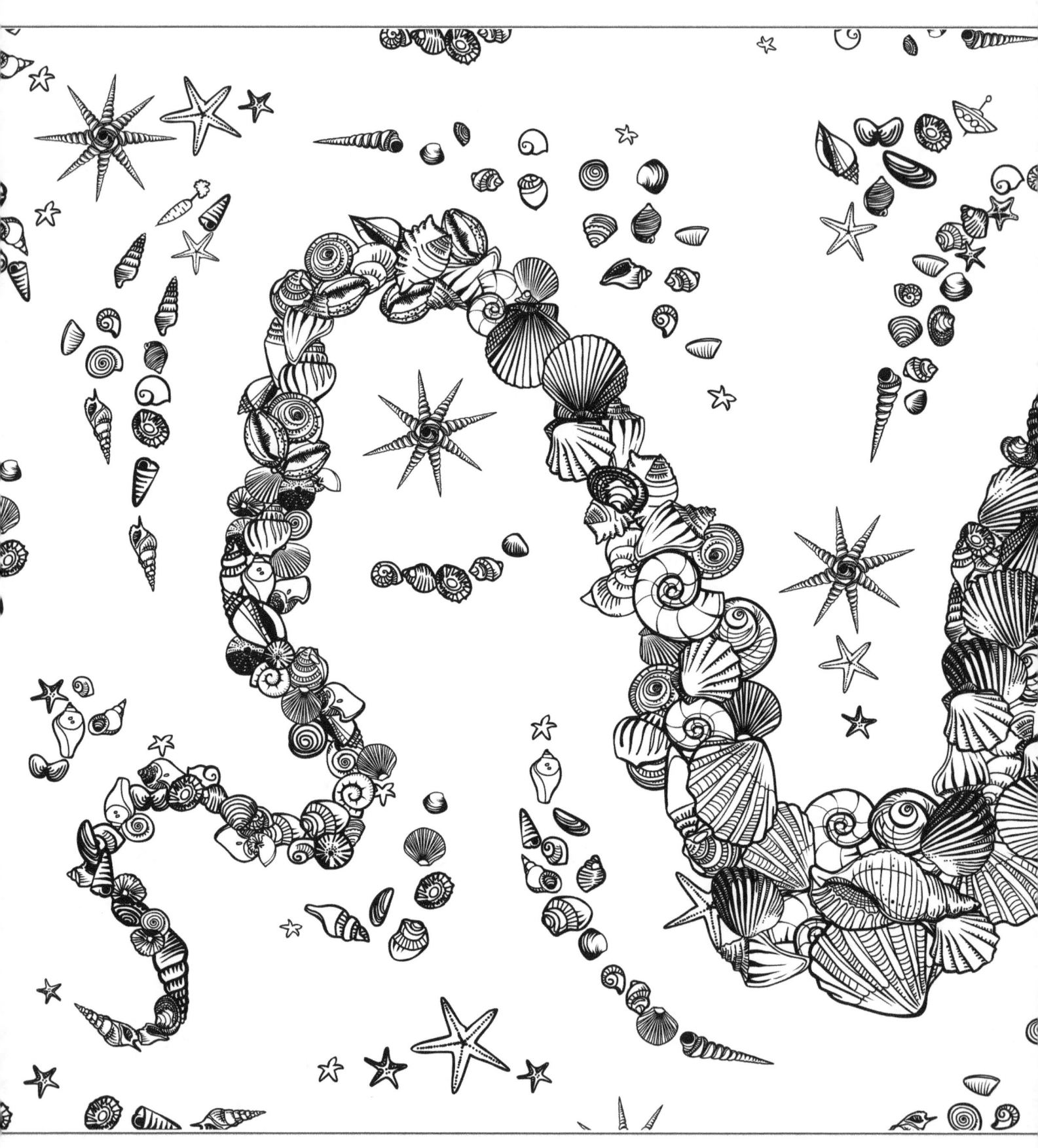

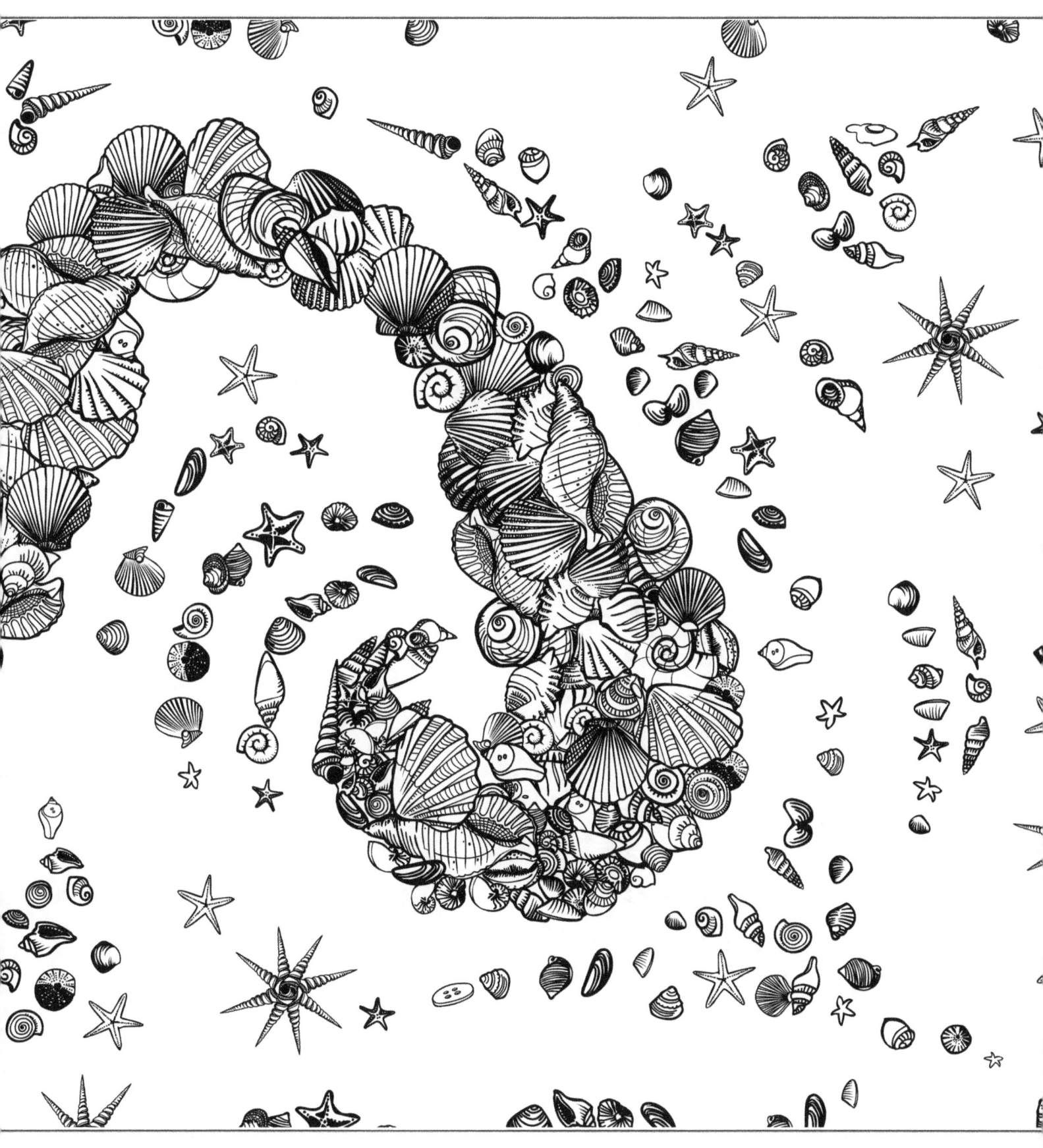

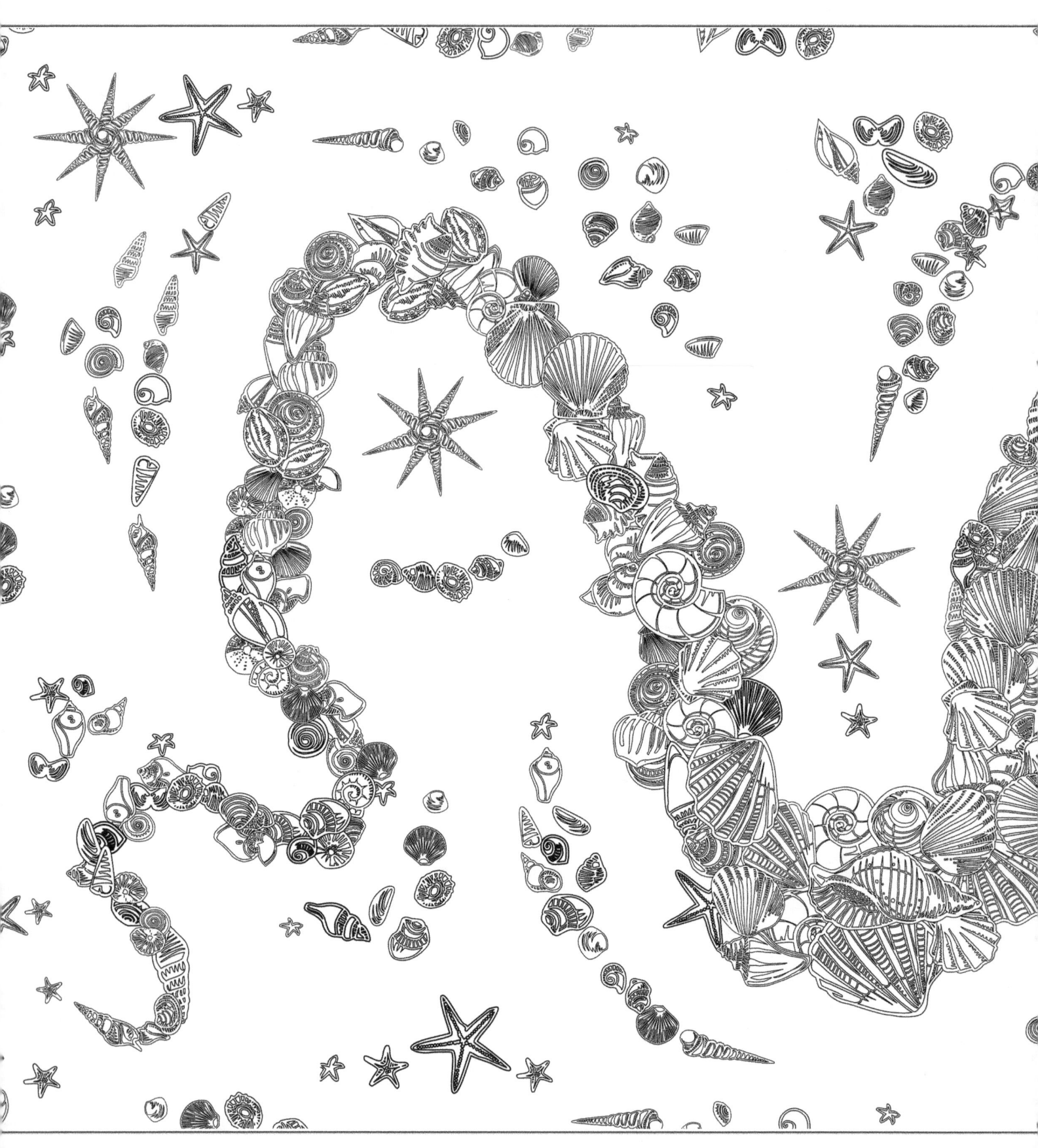

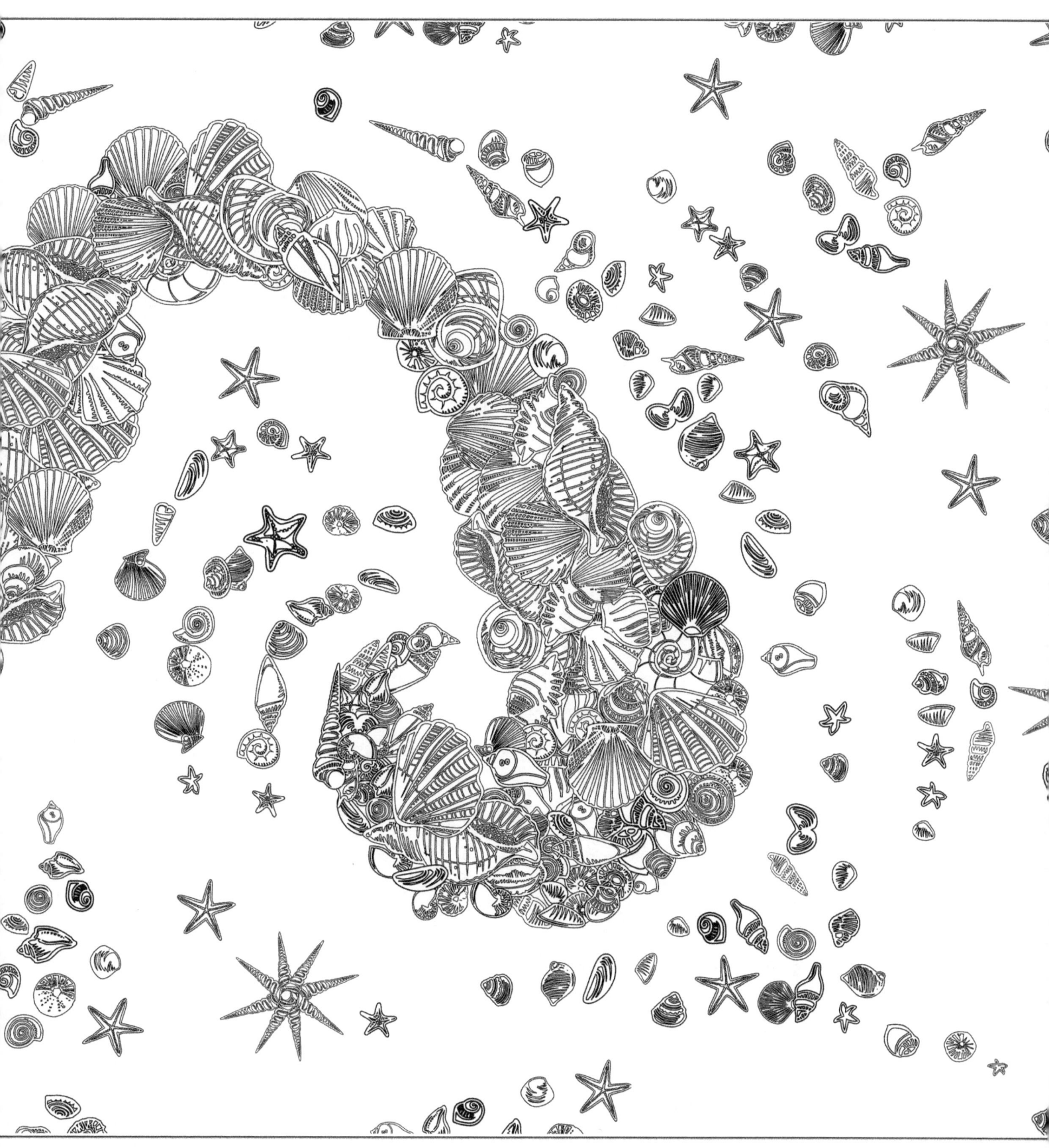

PART TWO

SOMETHING A BIT FISHY

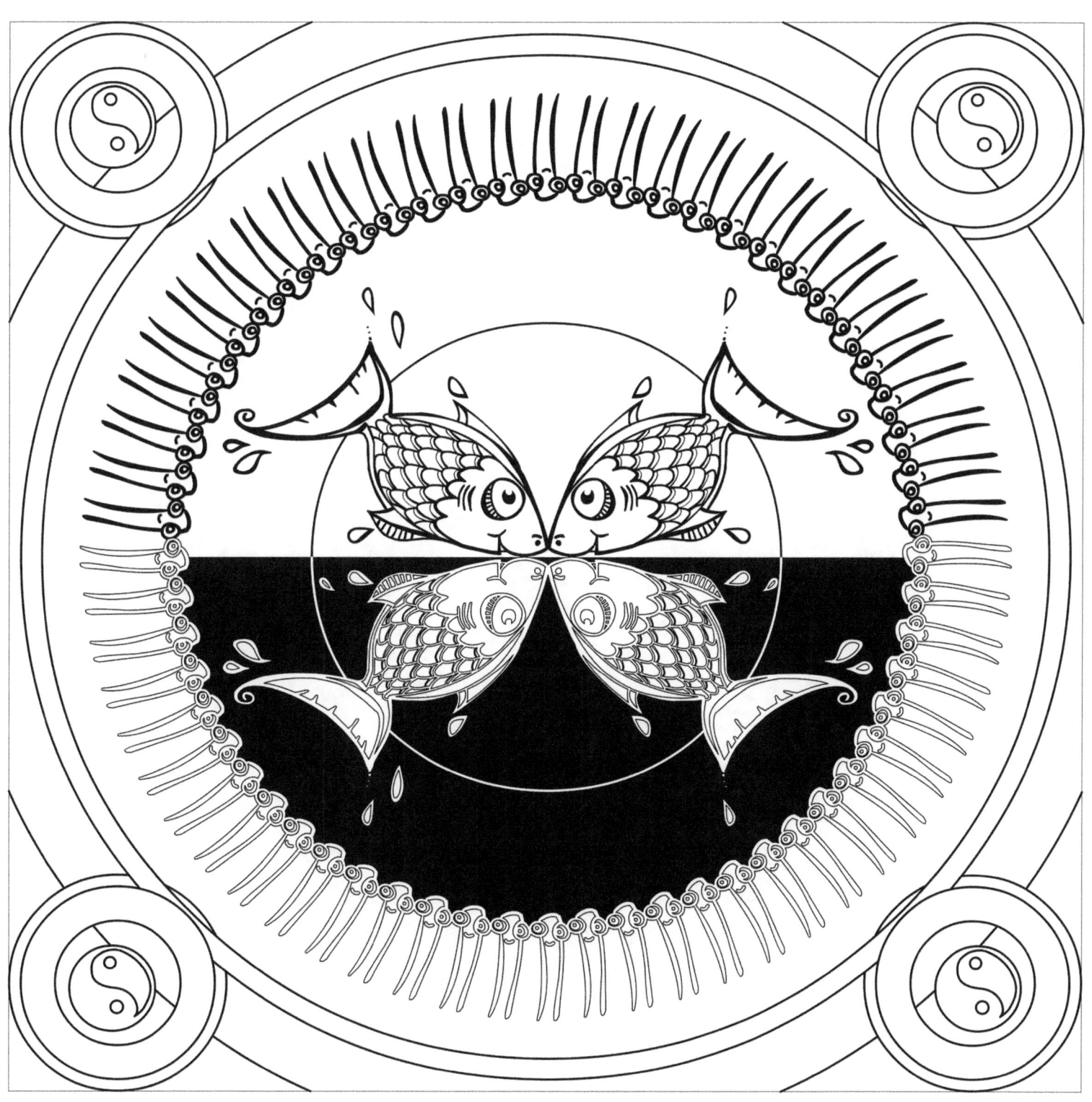

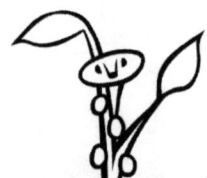

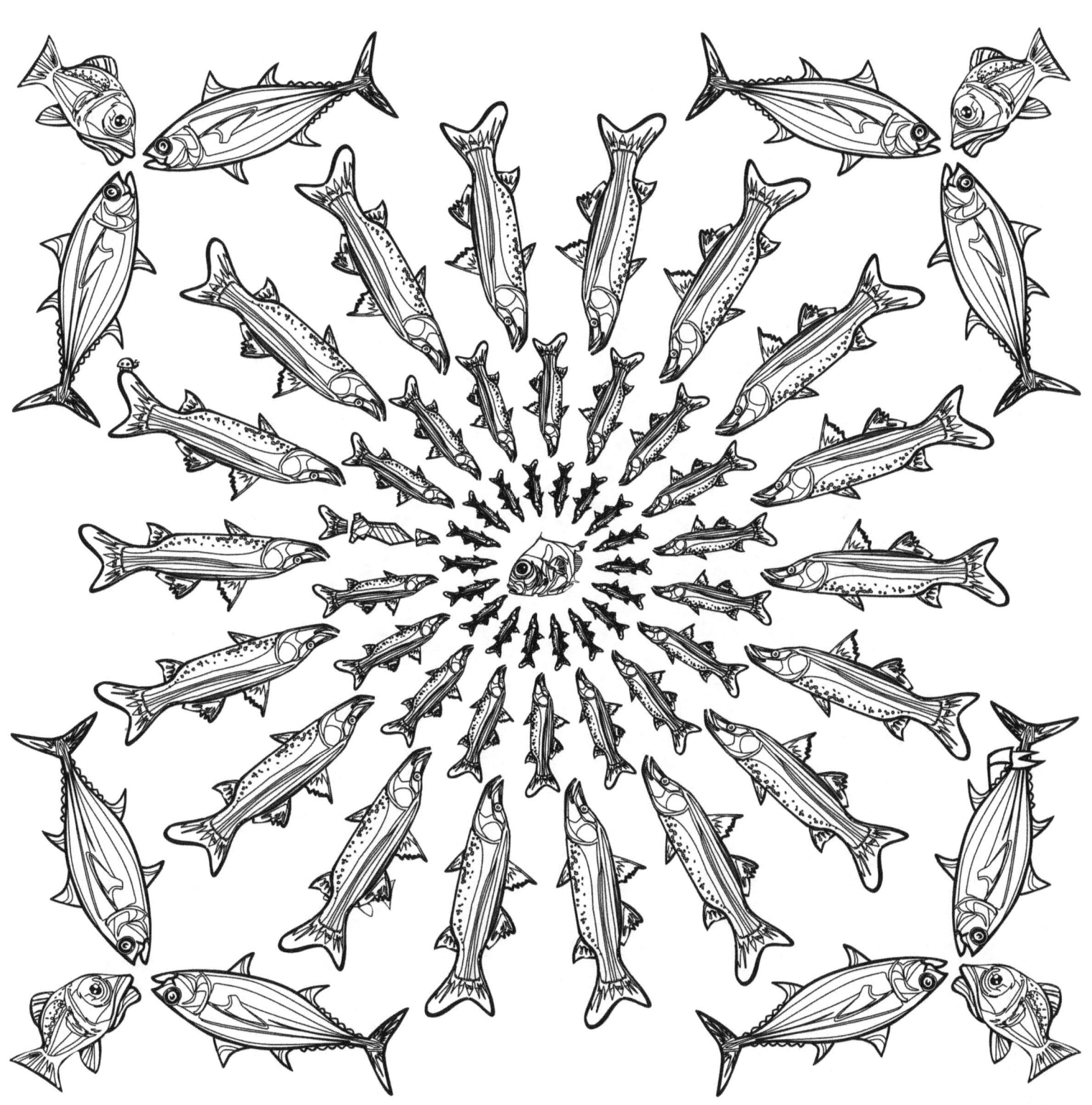

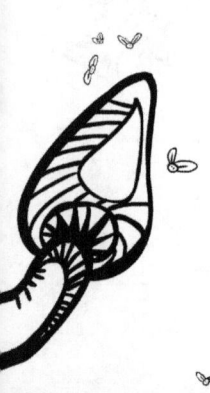

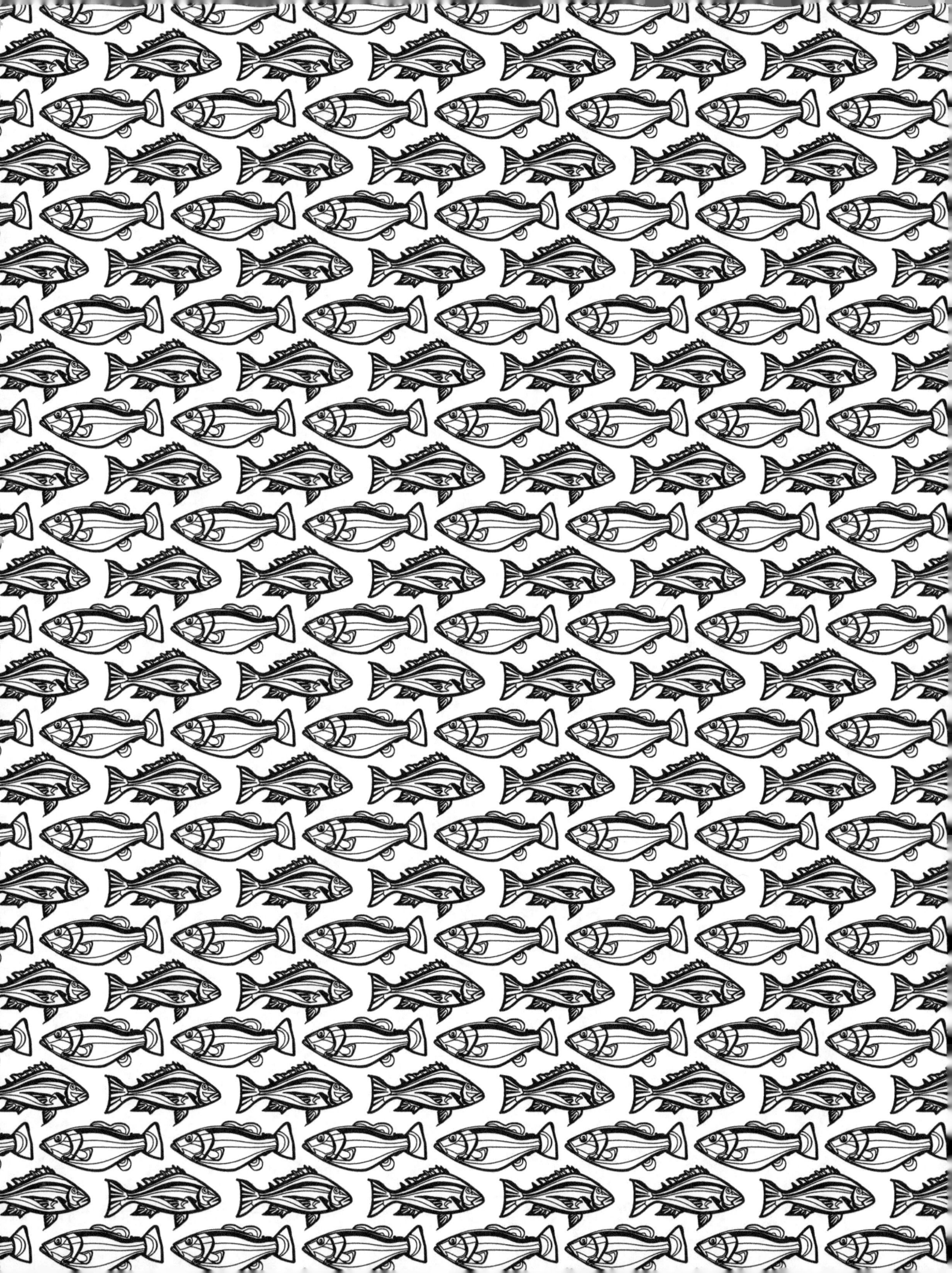

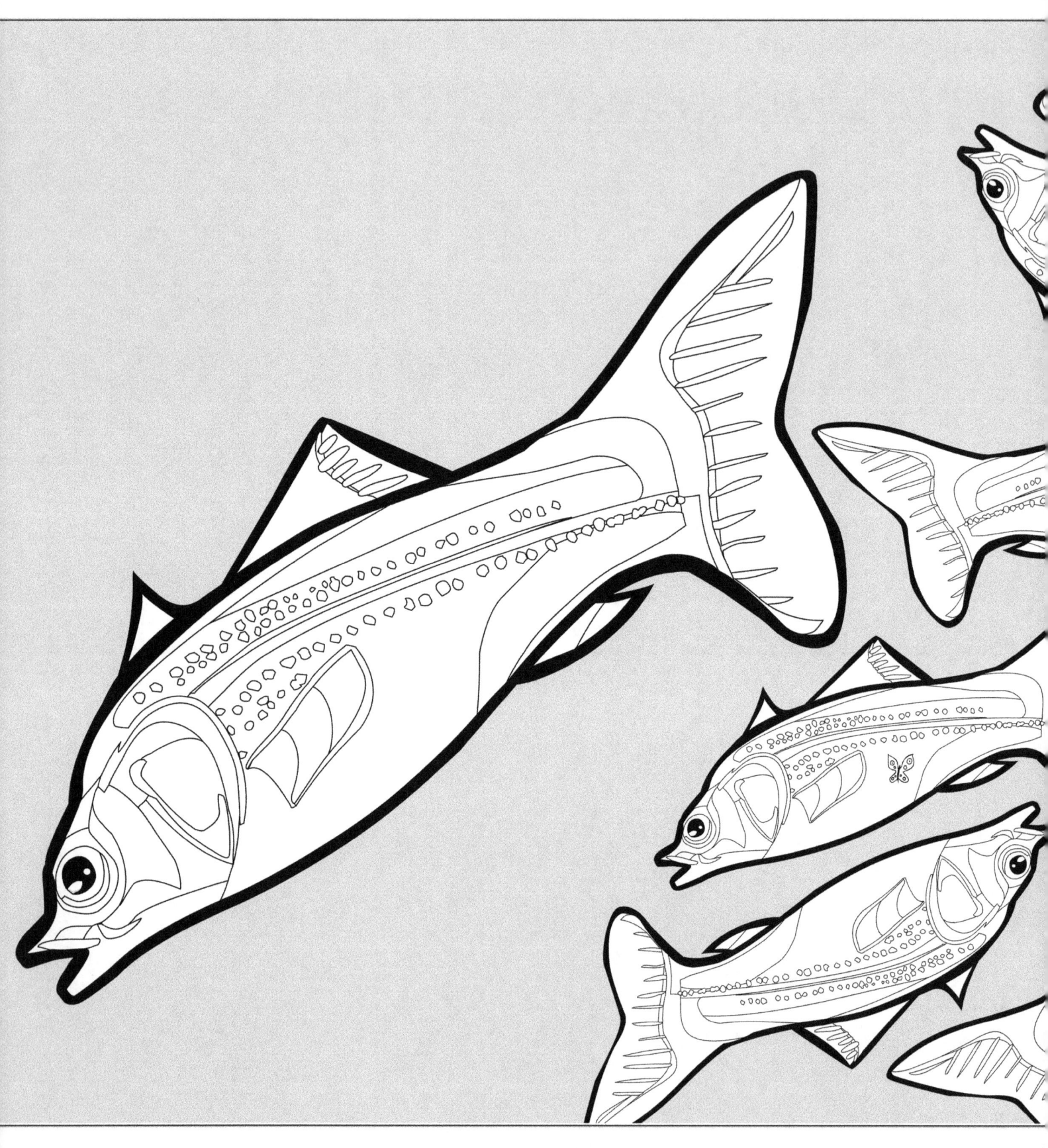

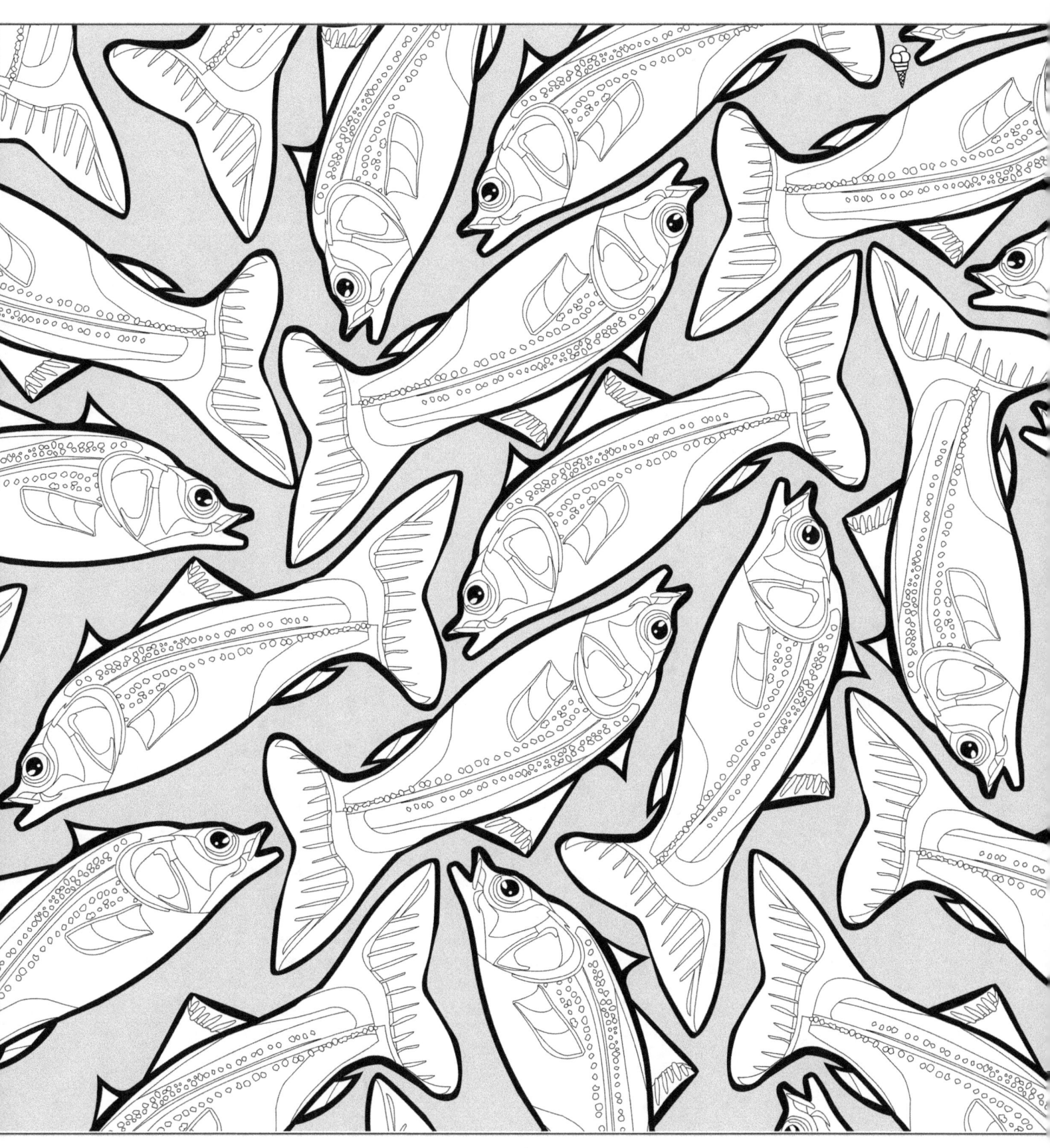

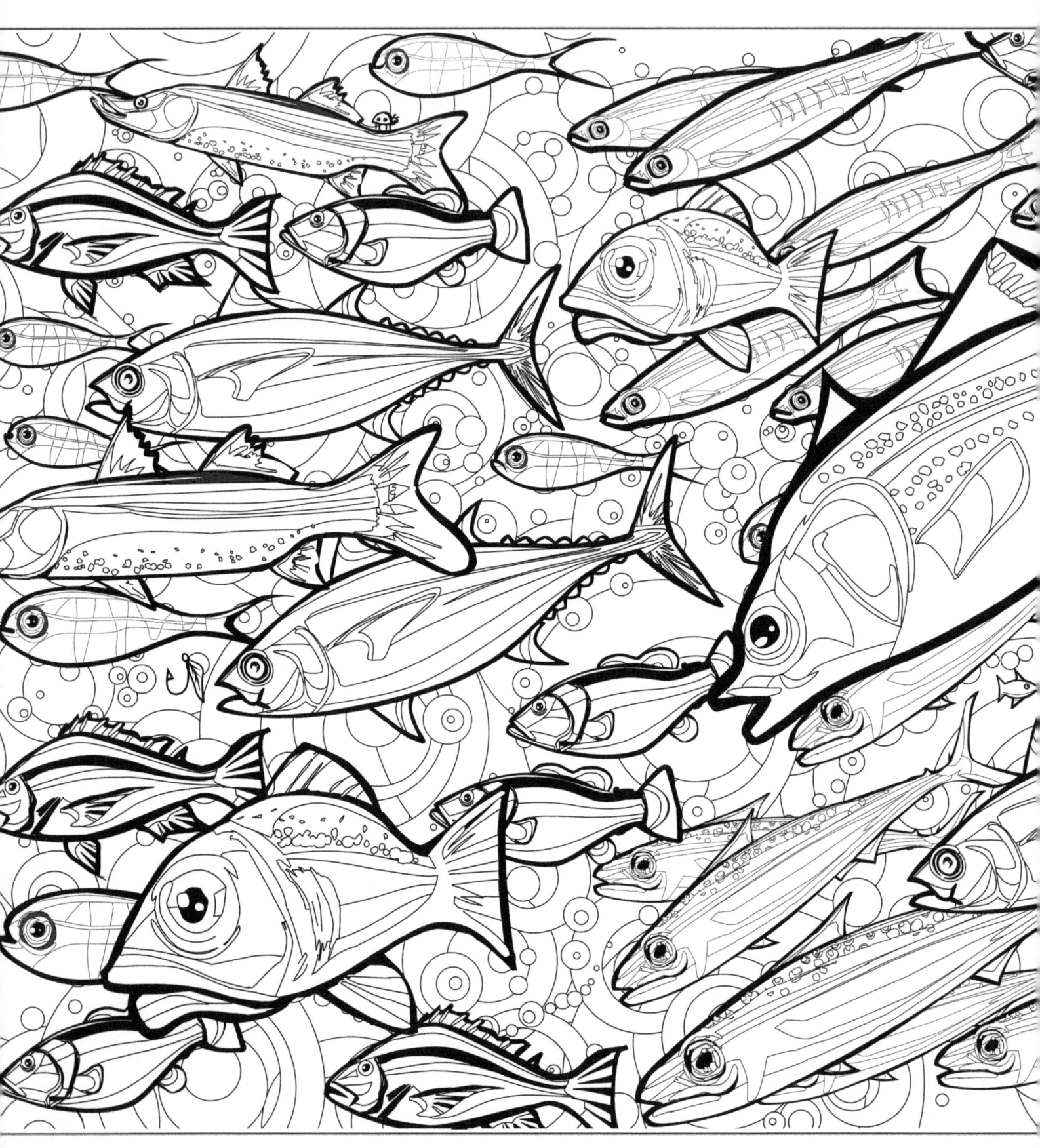

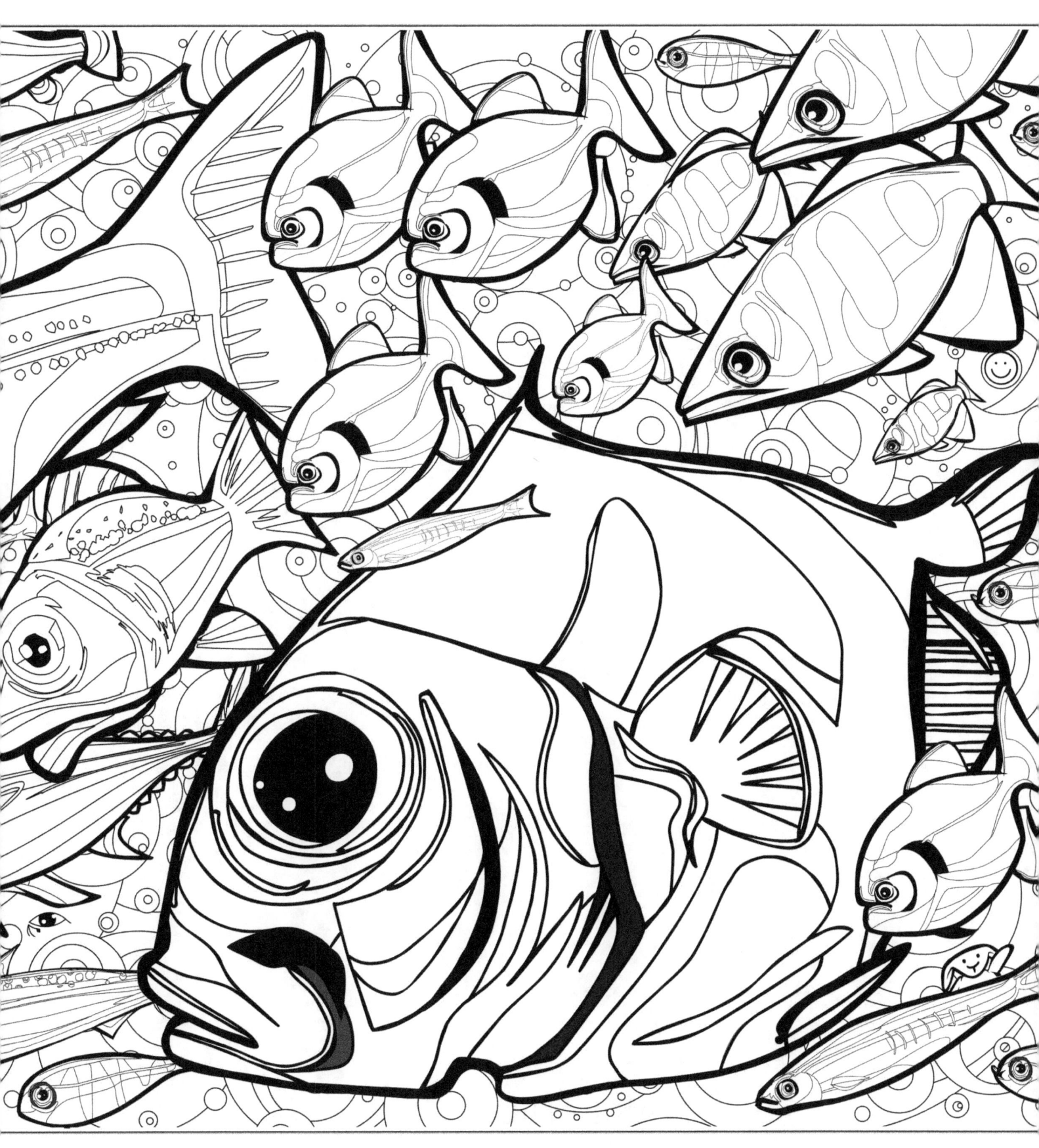

PART THREE

VERSATILE FOREST

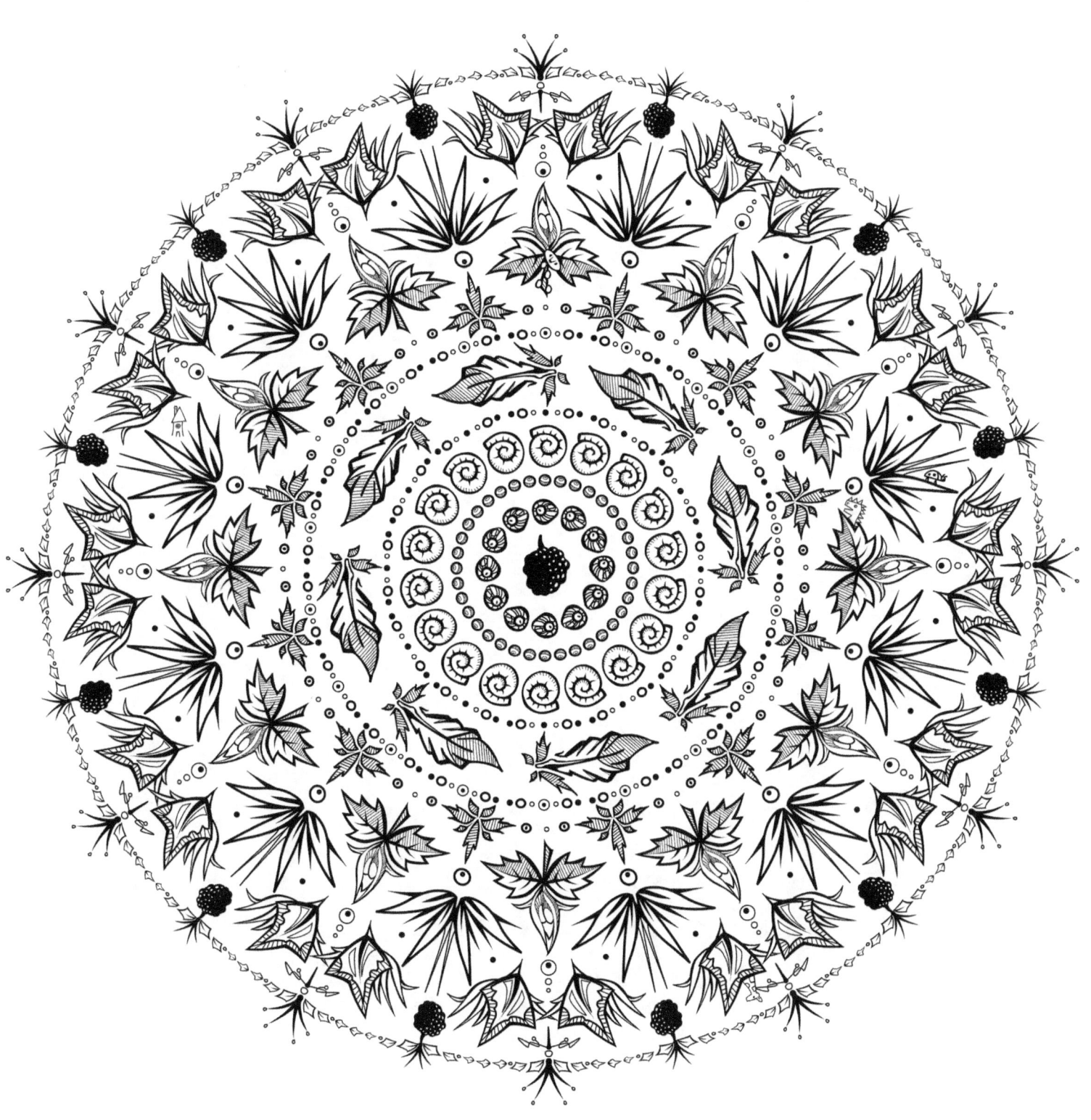

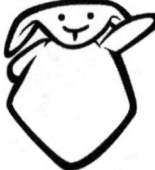

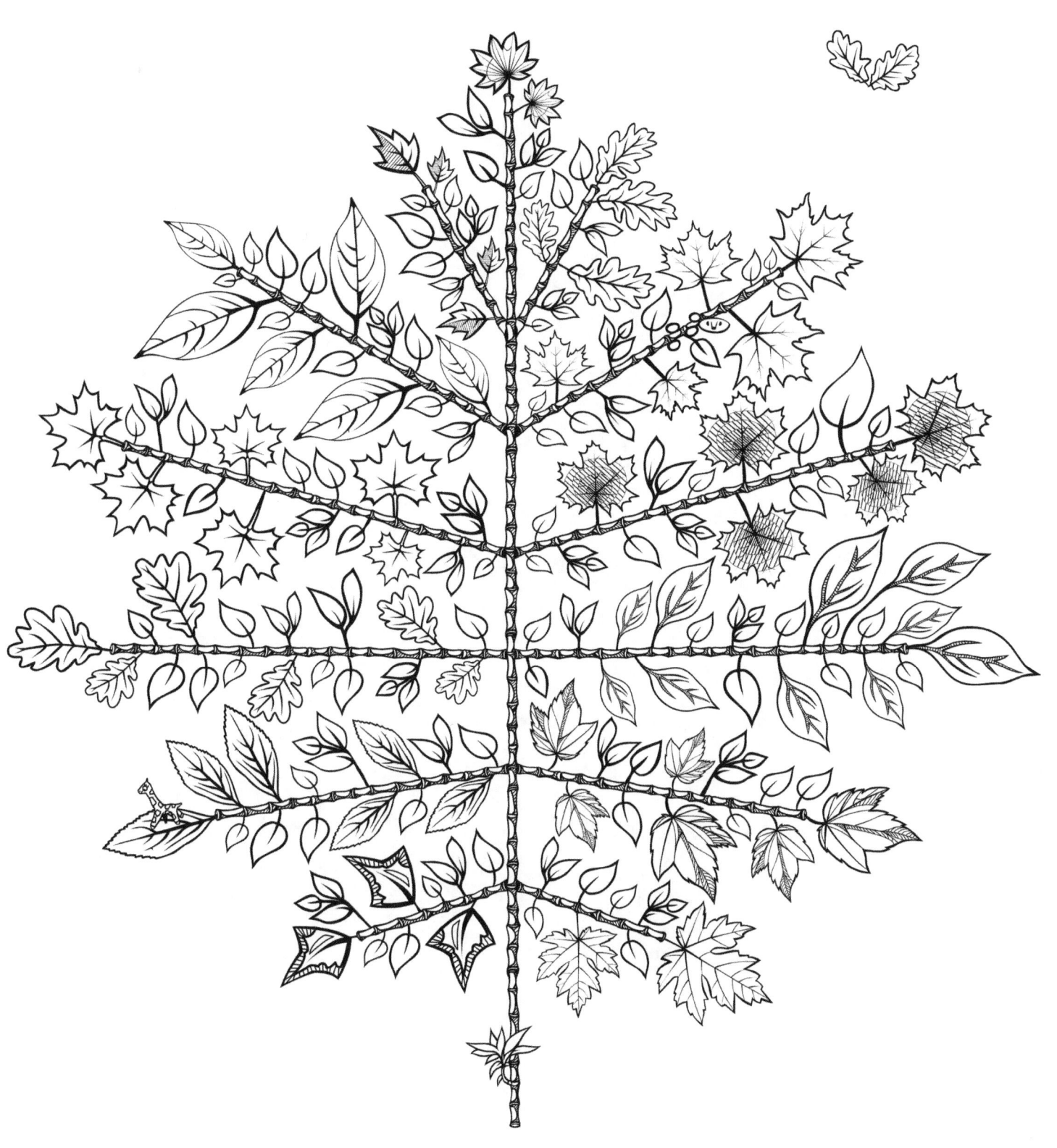

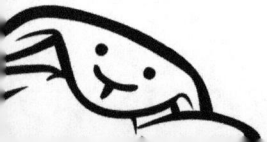

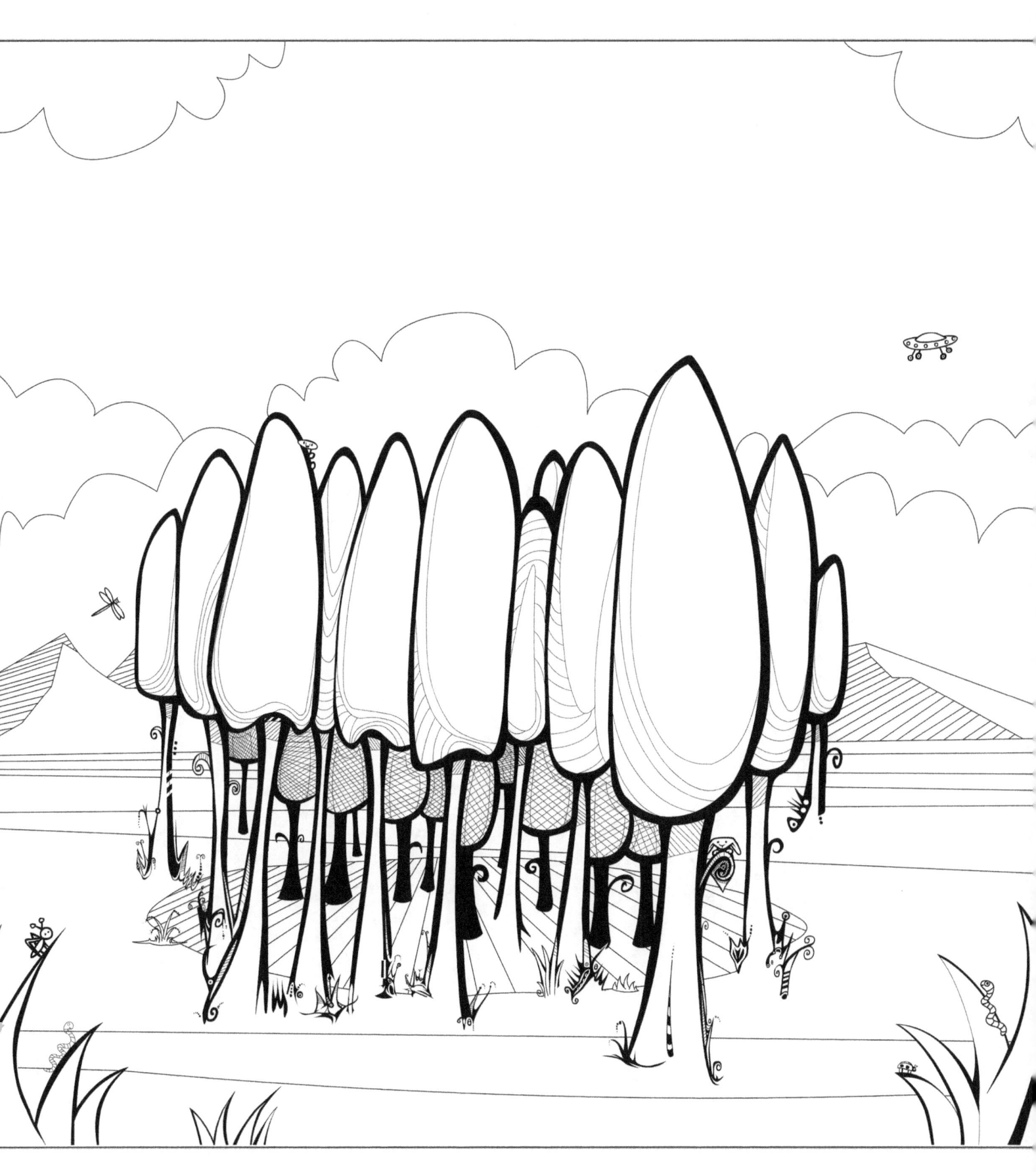

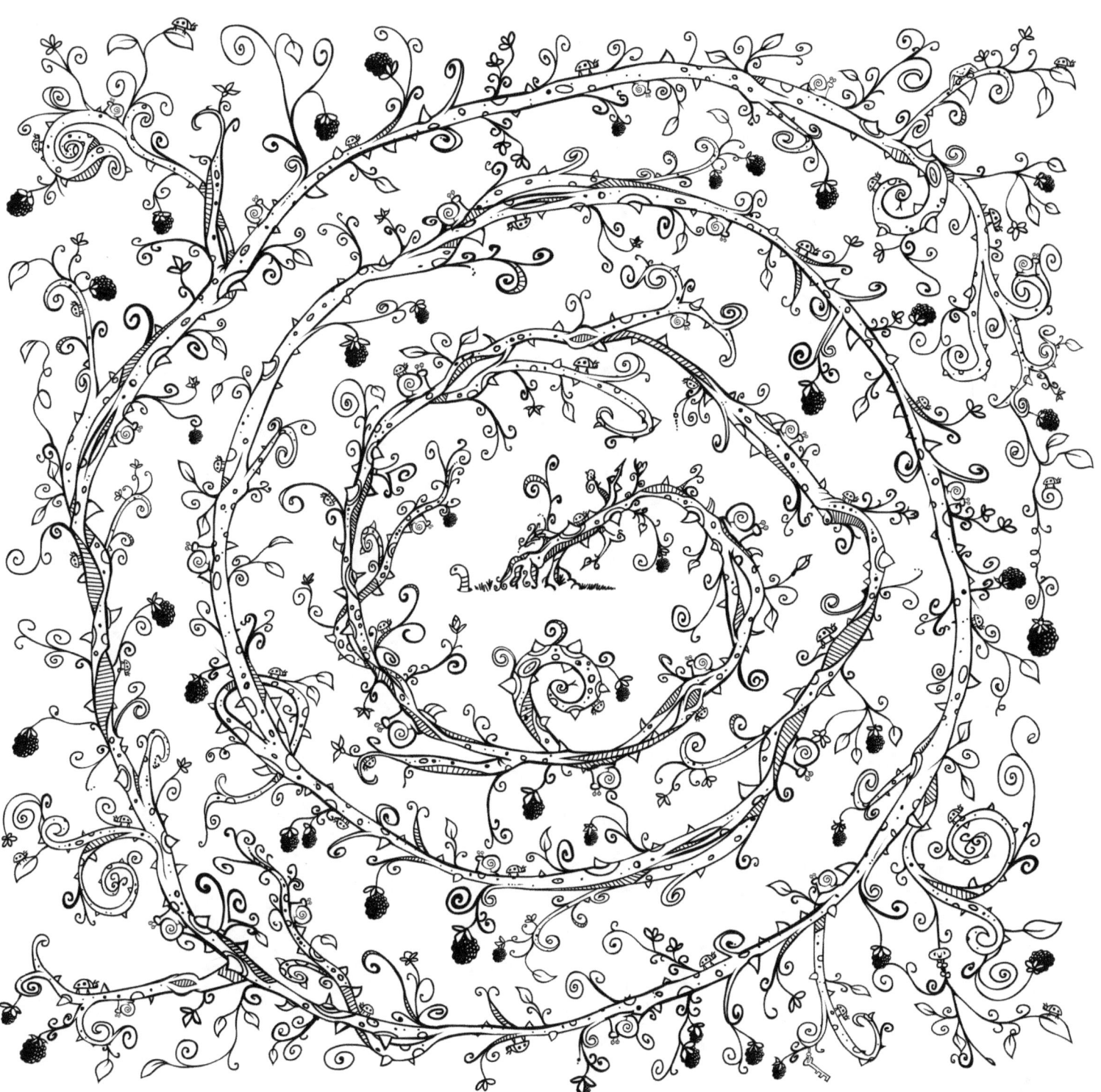

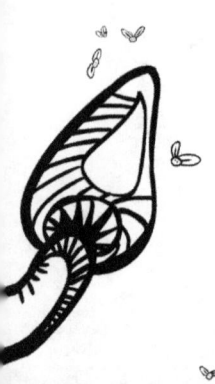

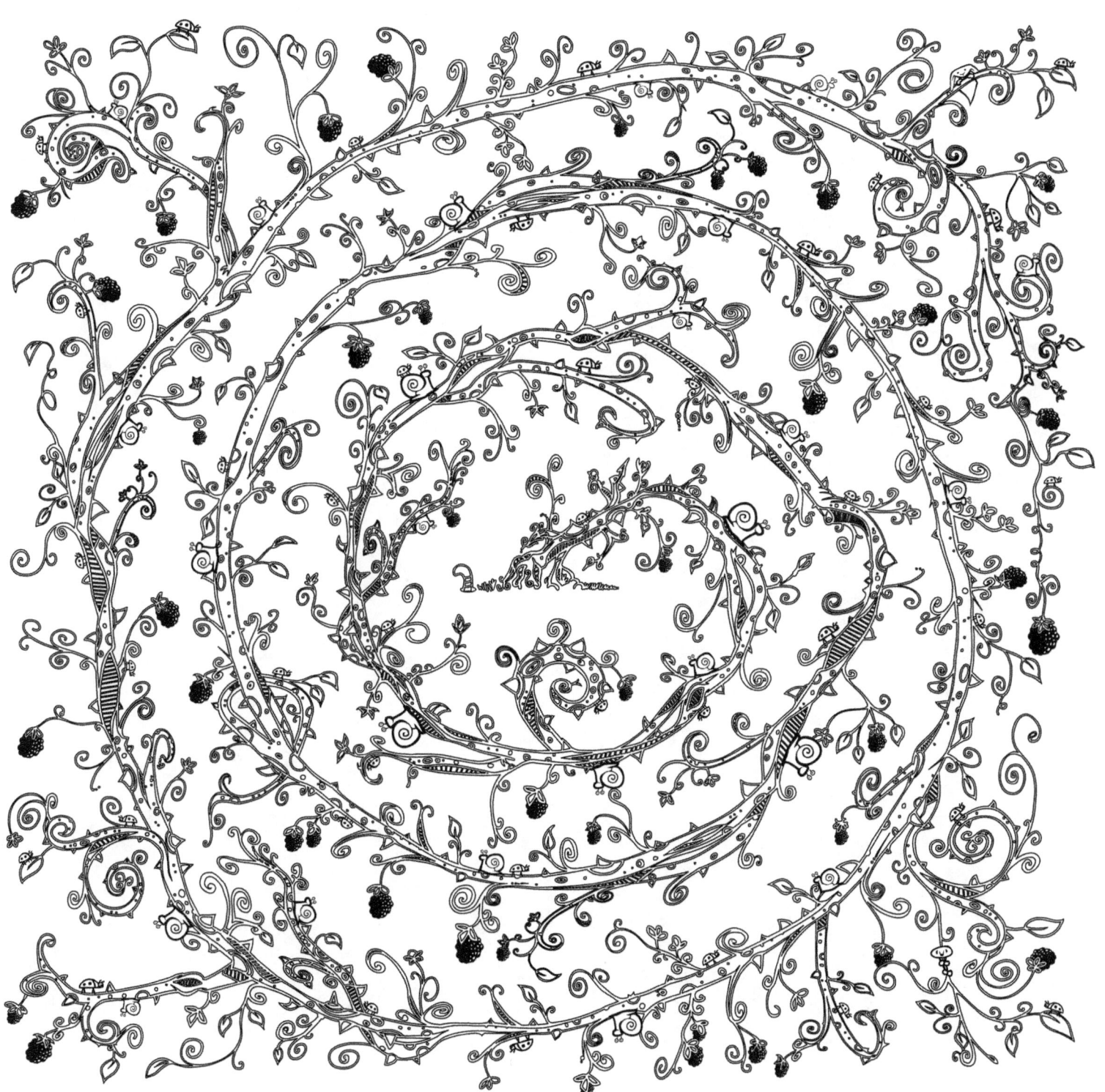

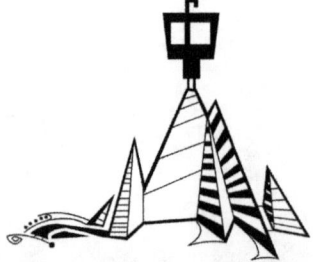

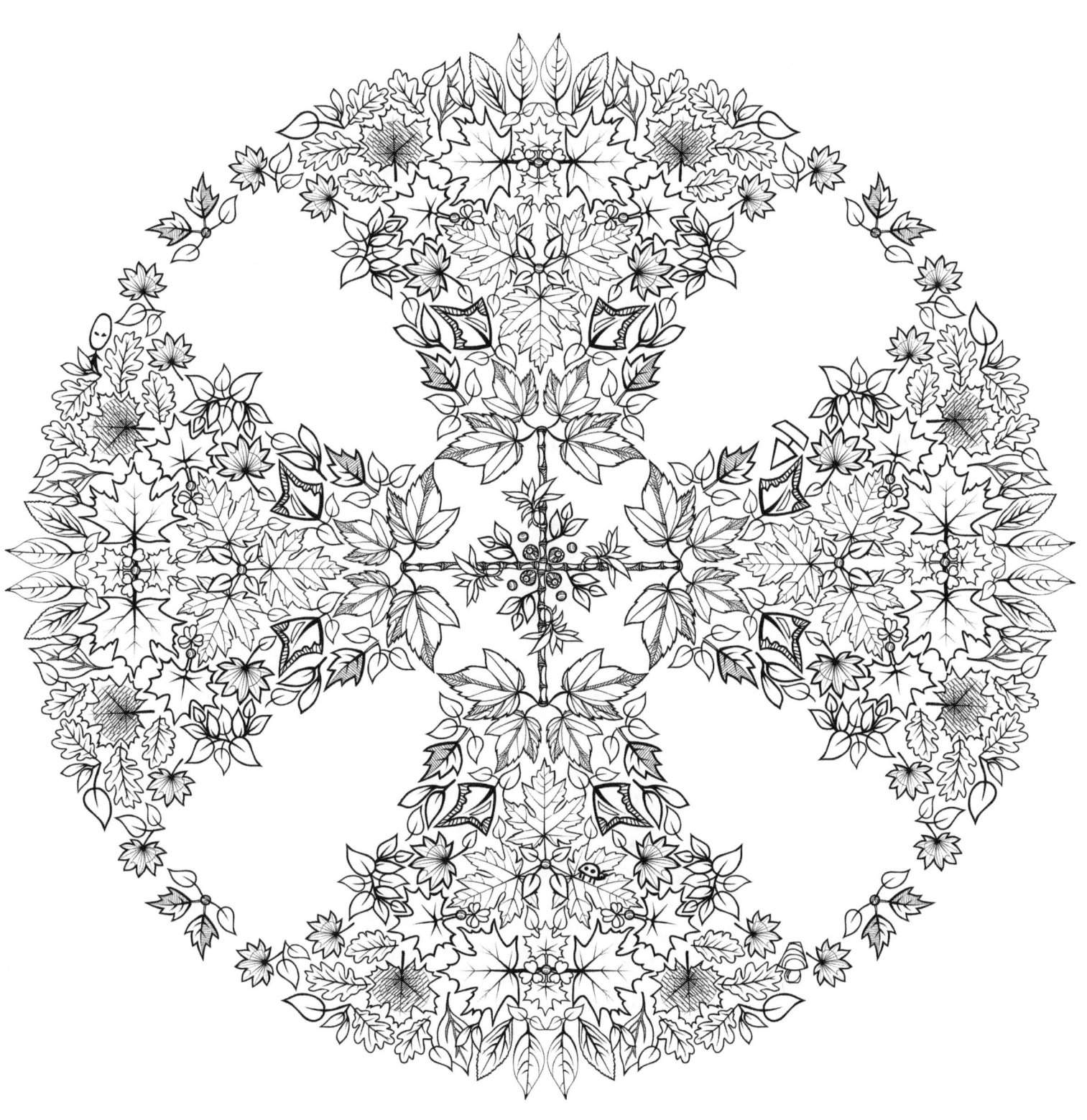

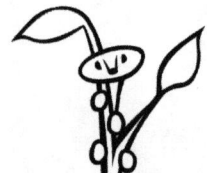

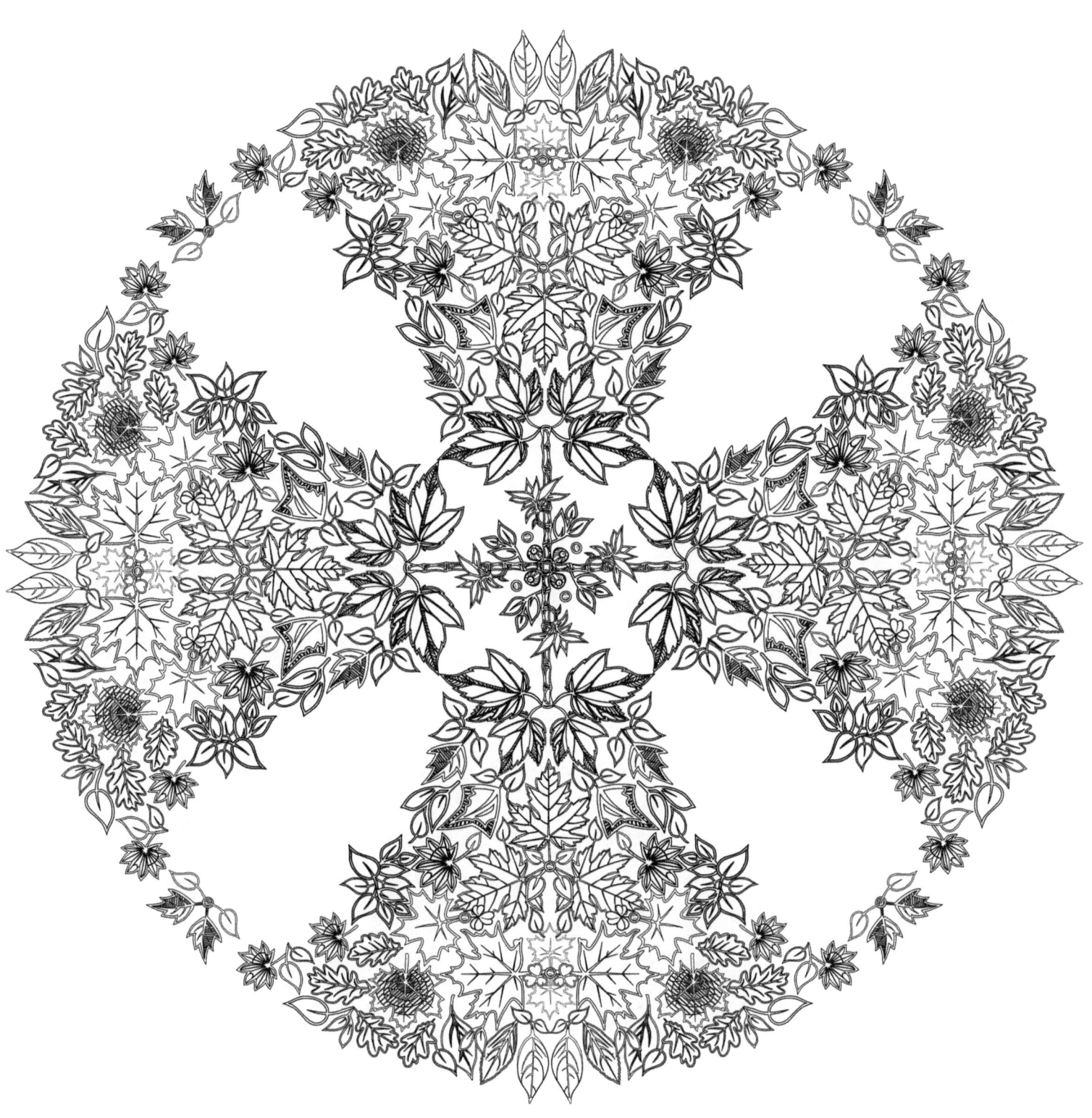

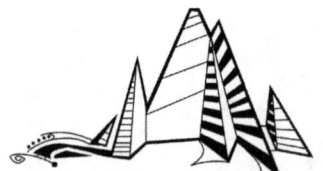

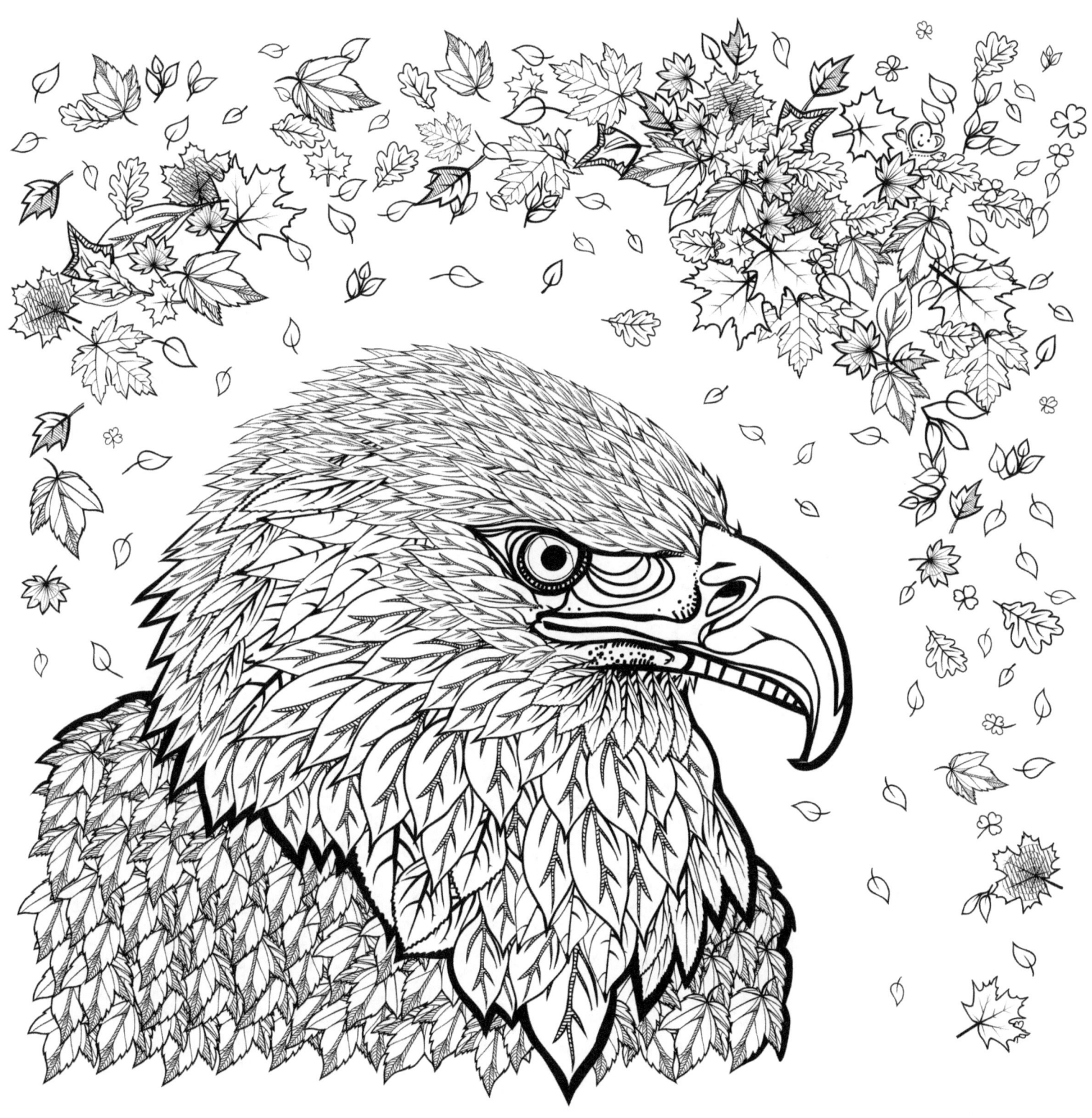

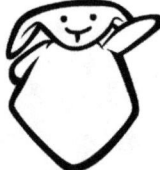

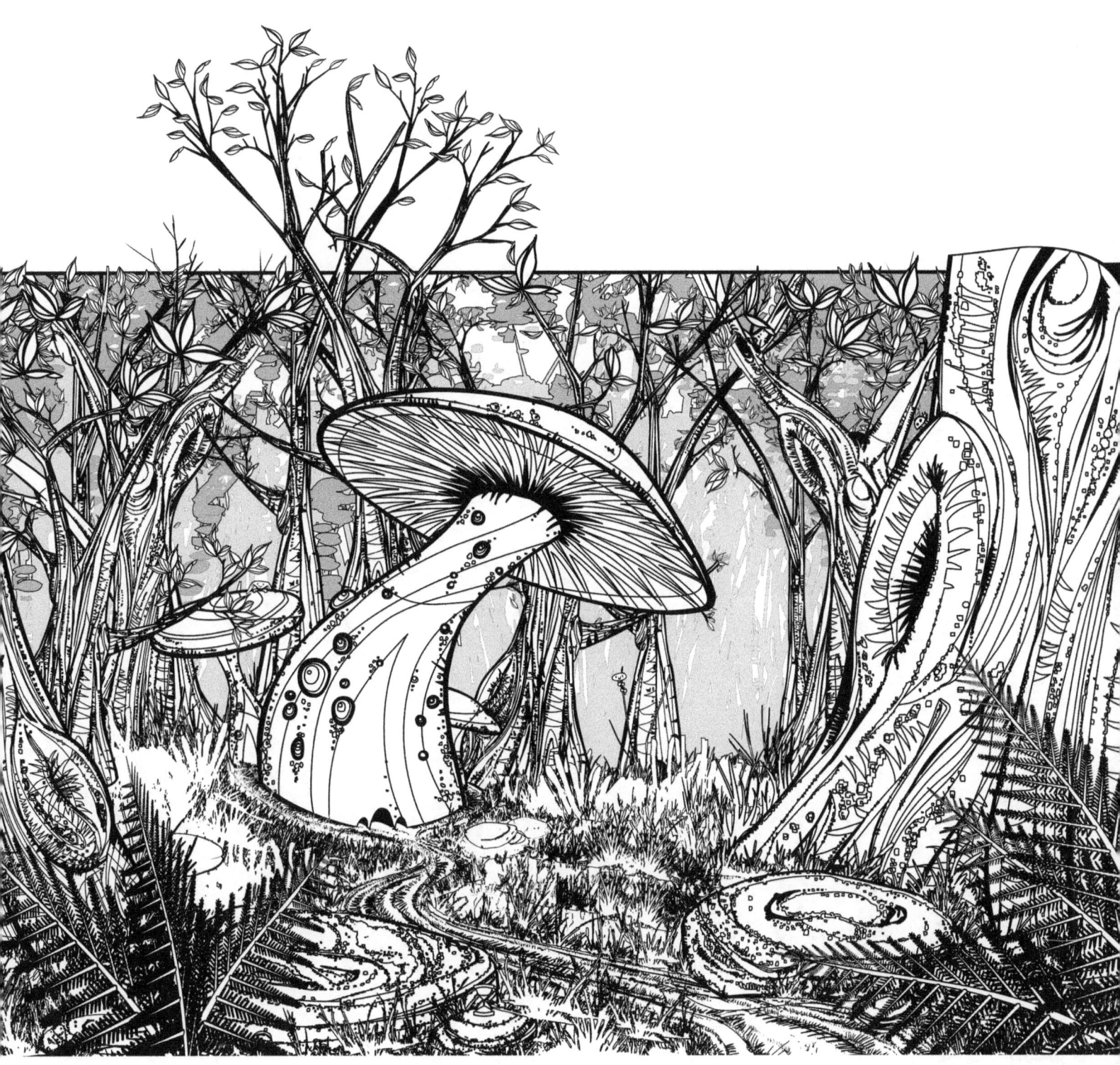

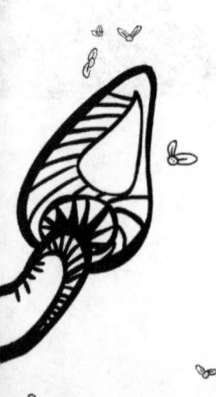

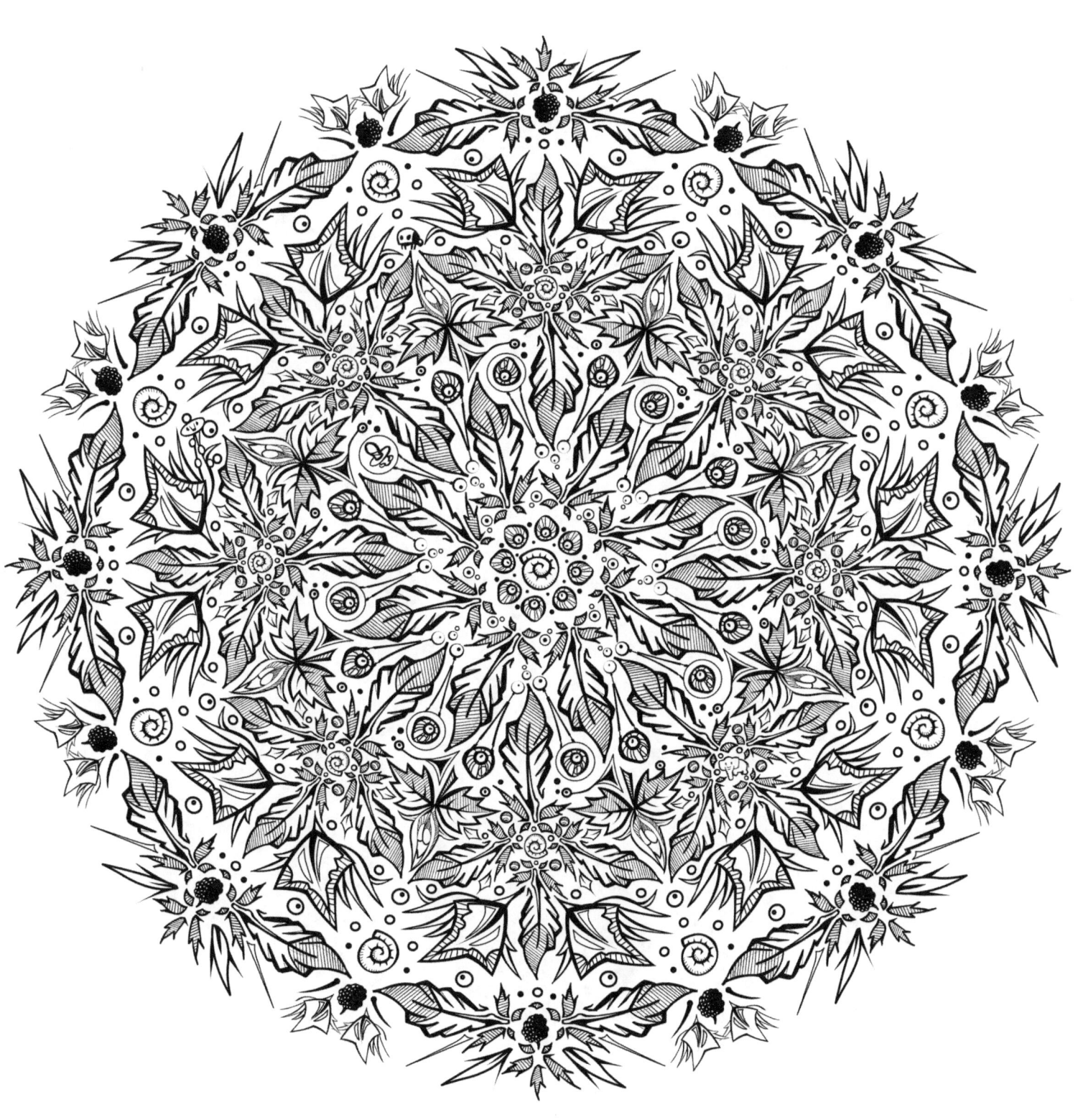

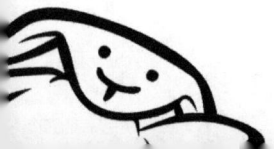

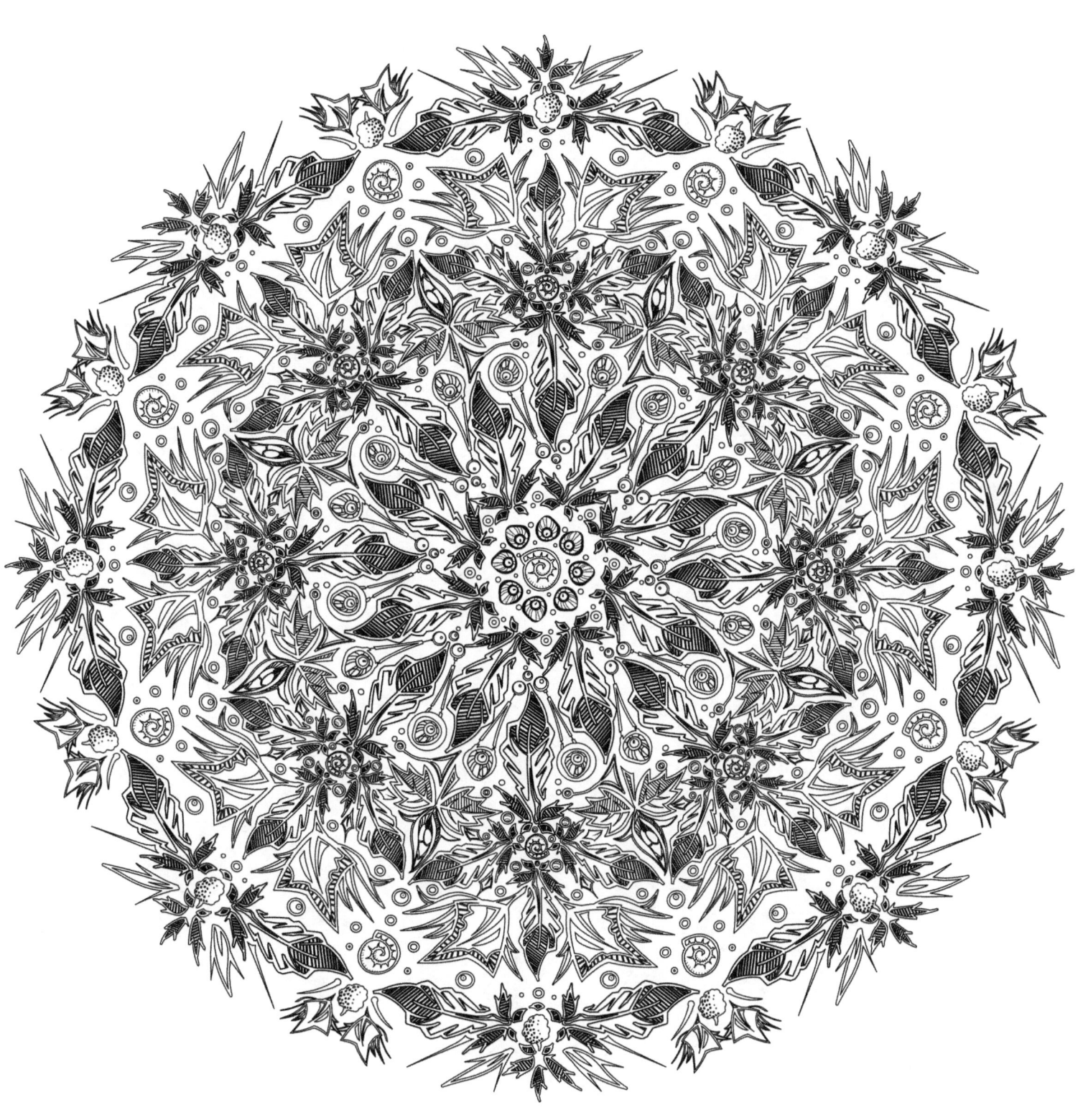

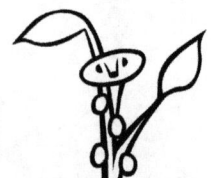

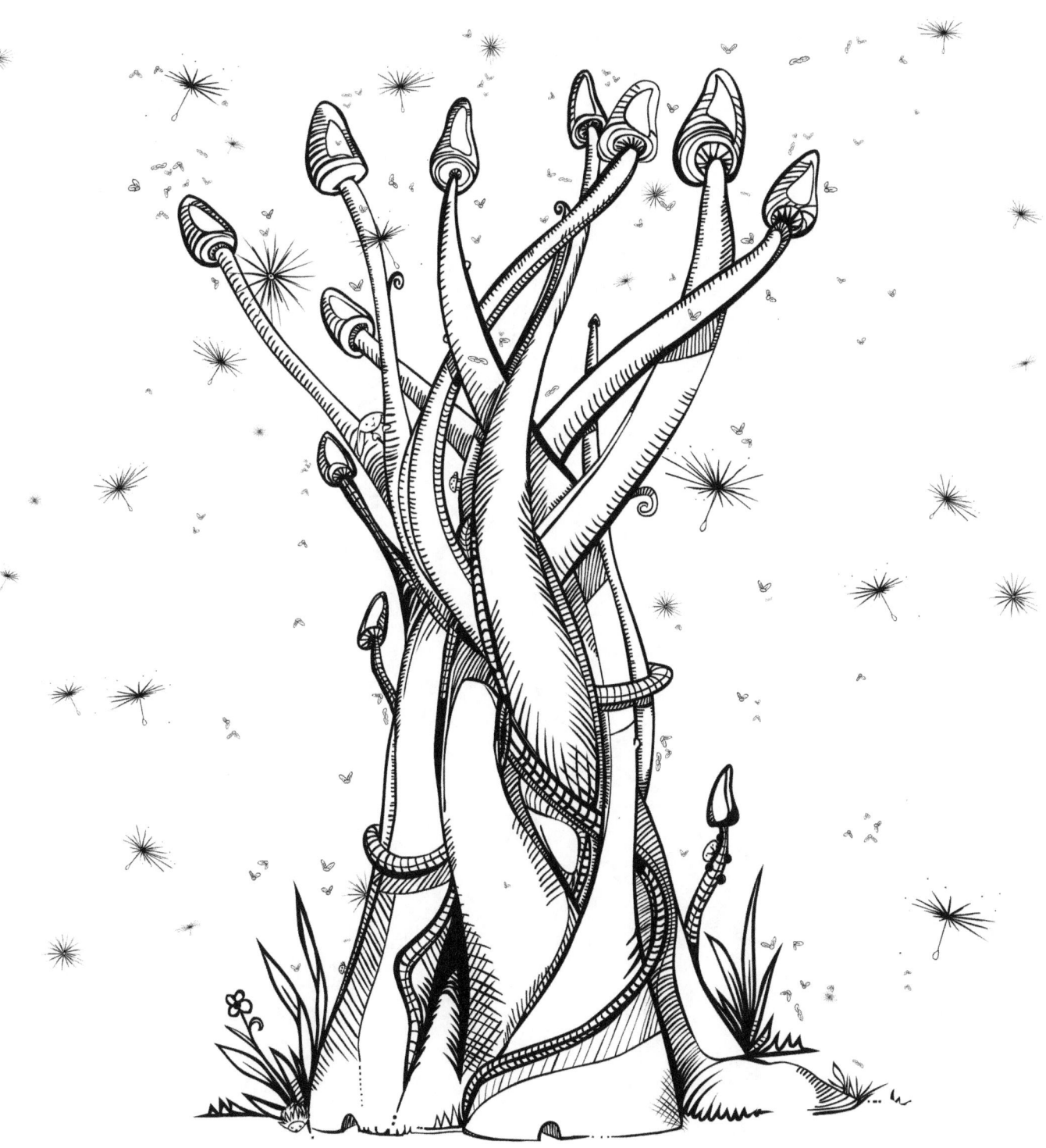

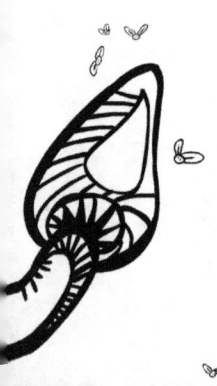

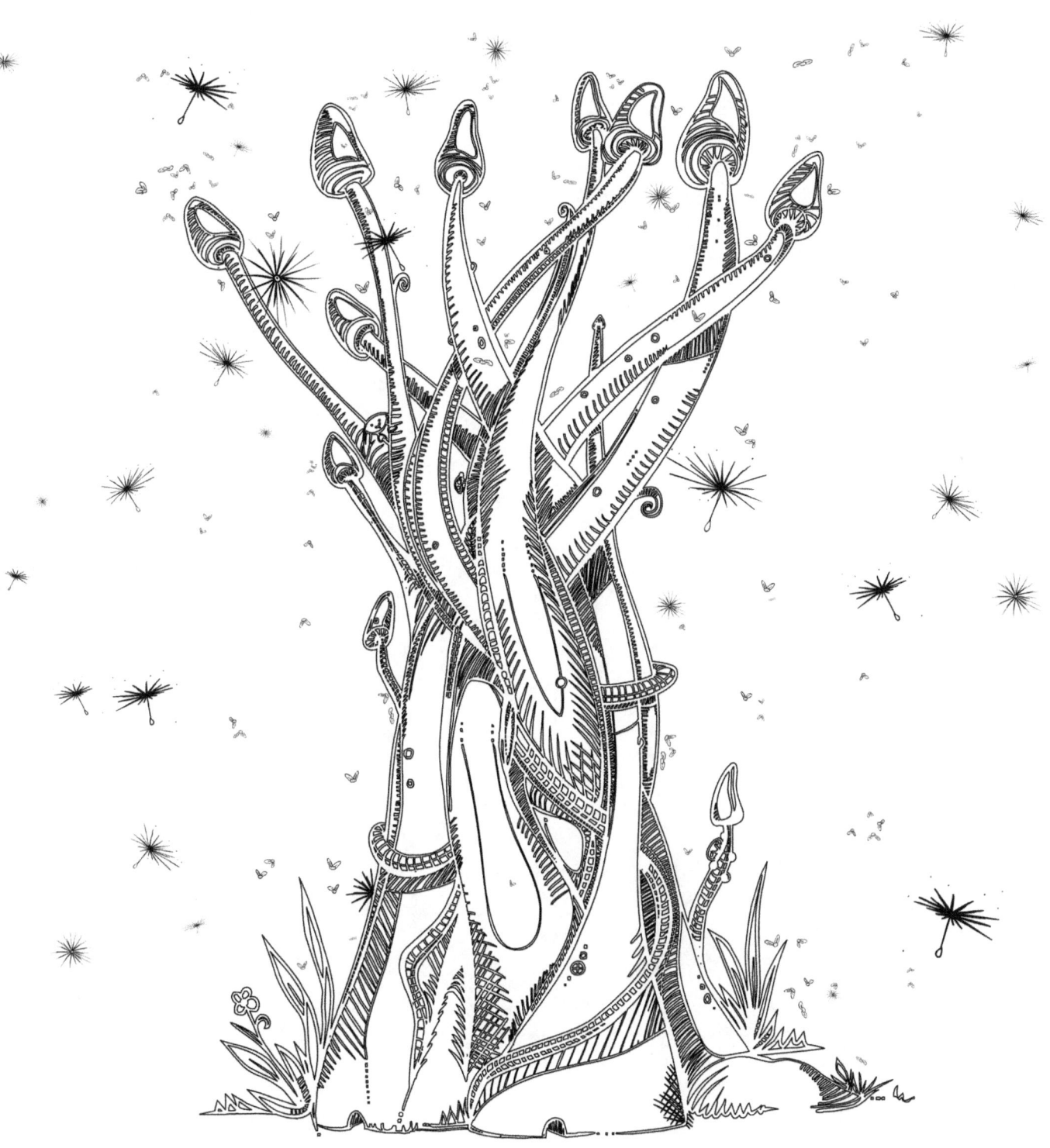

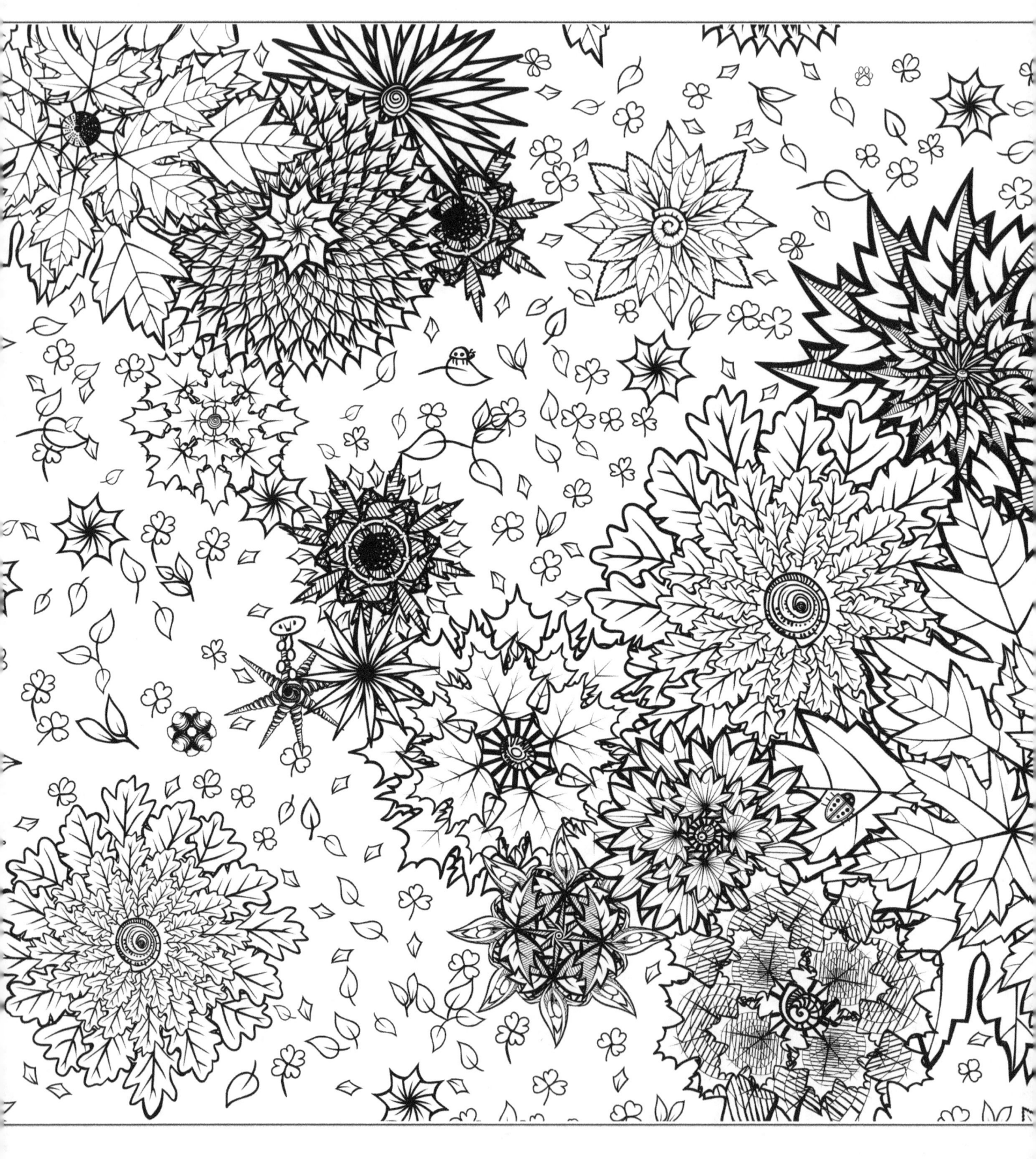

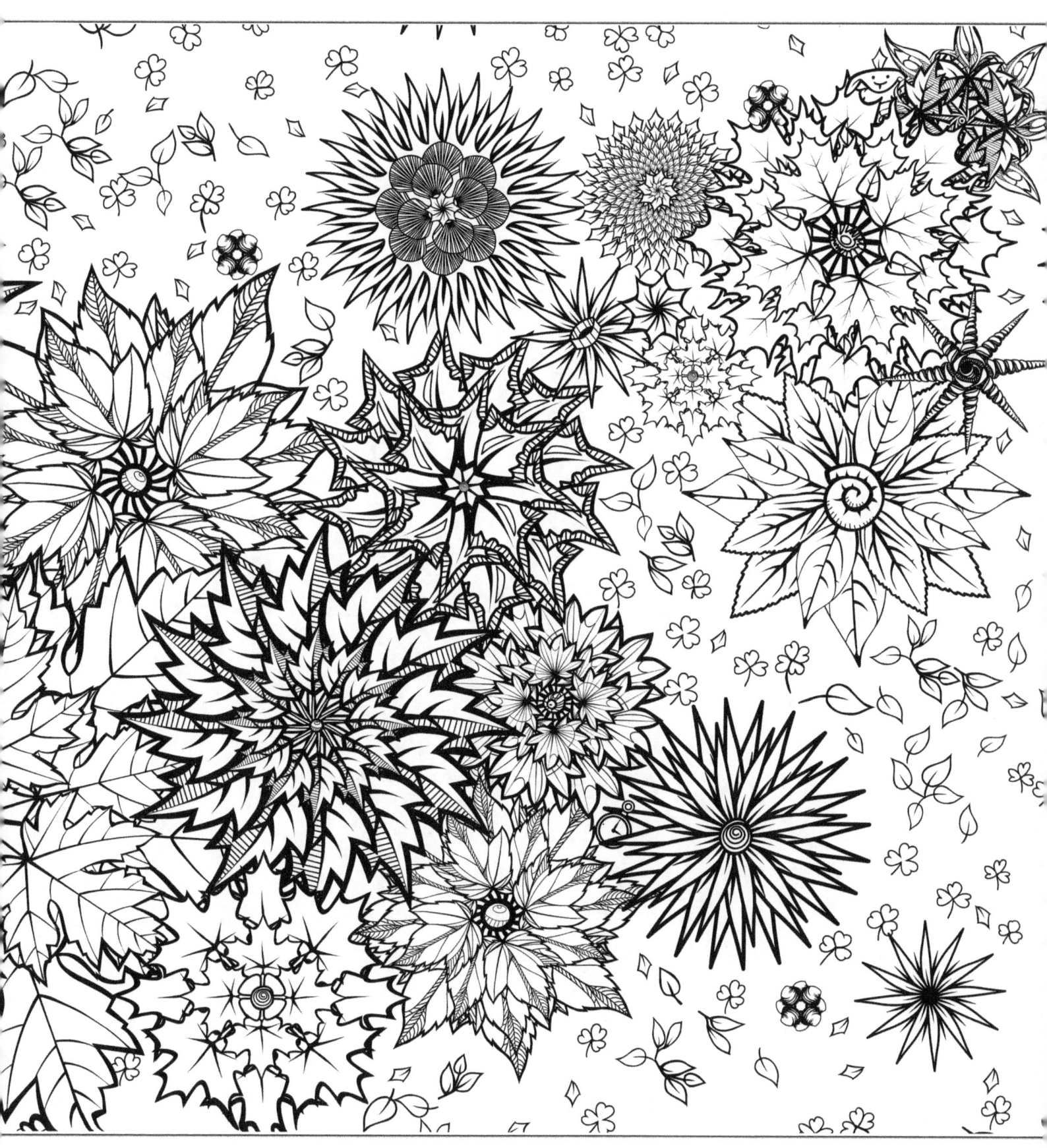

PART FOUR

FLOREALY INTRICATE   >>

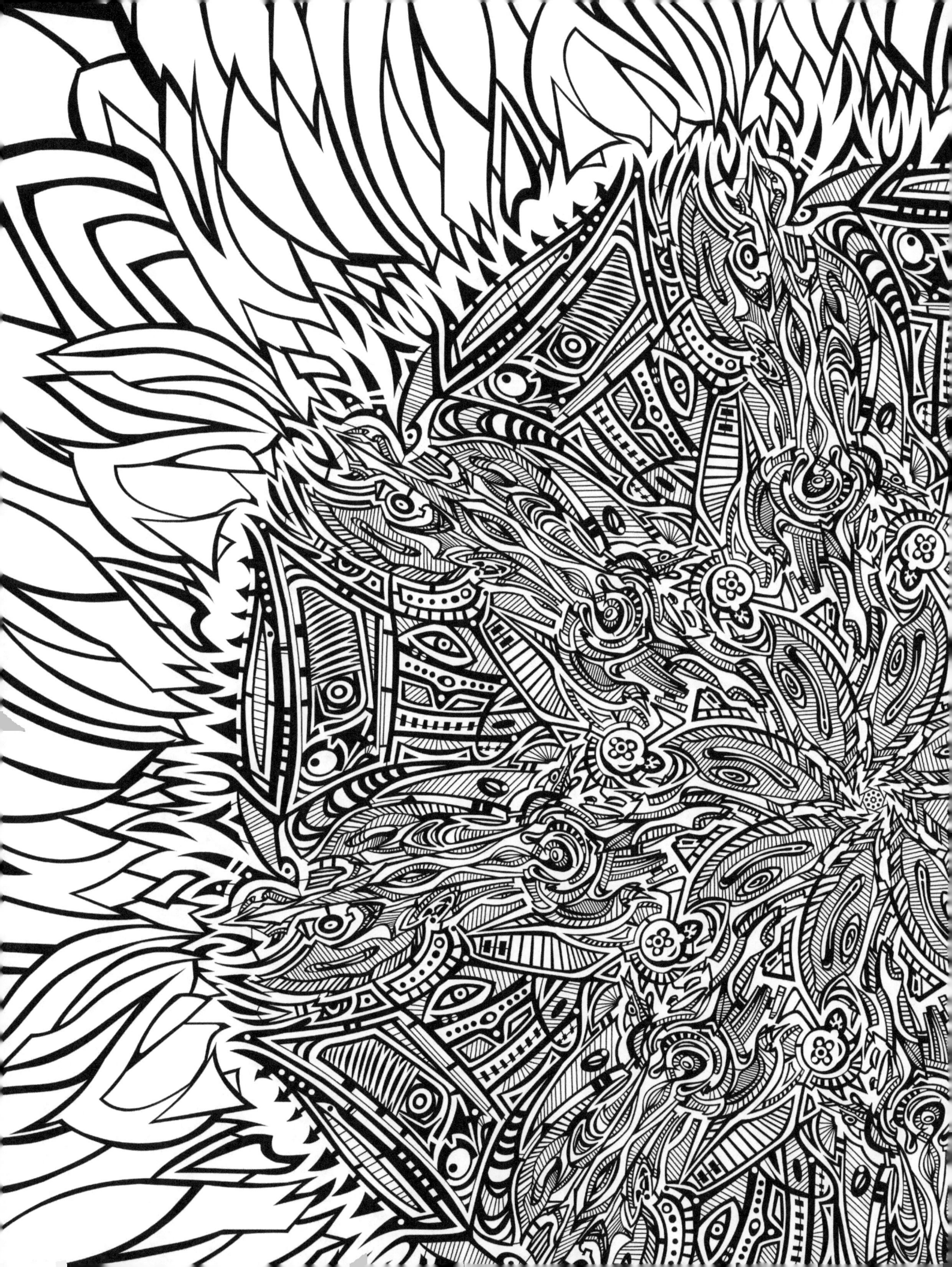

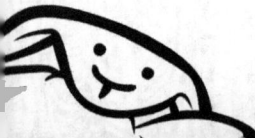

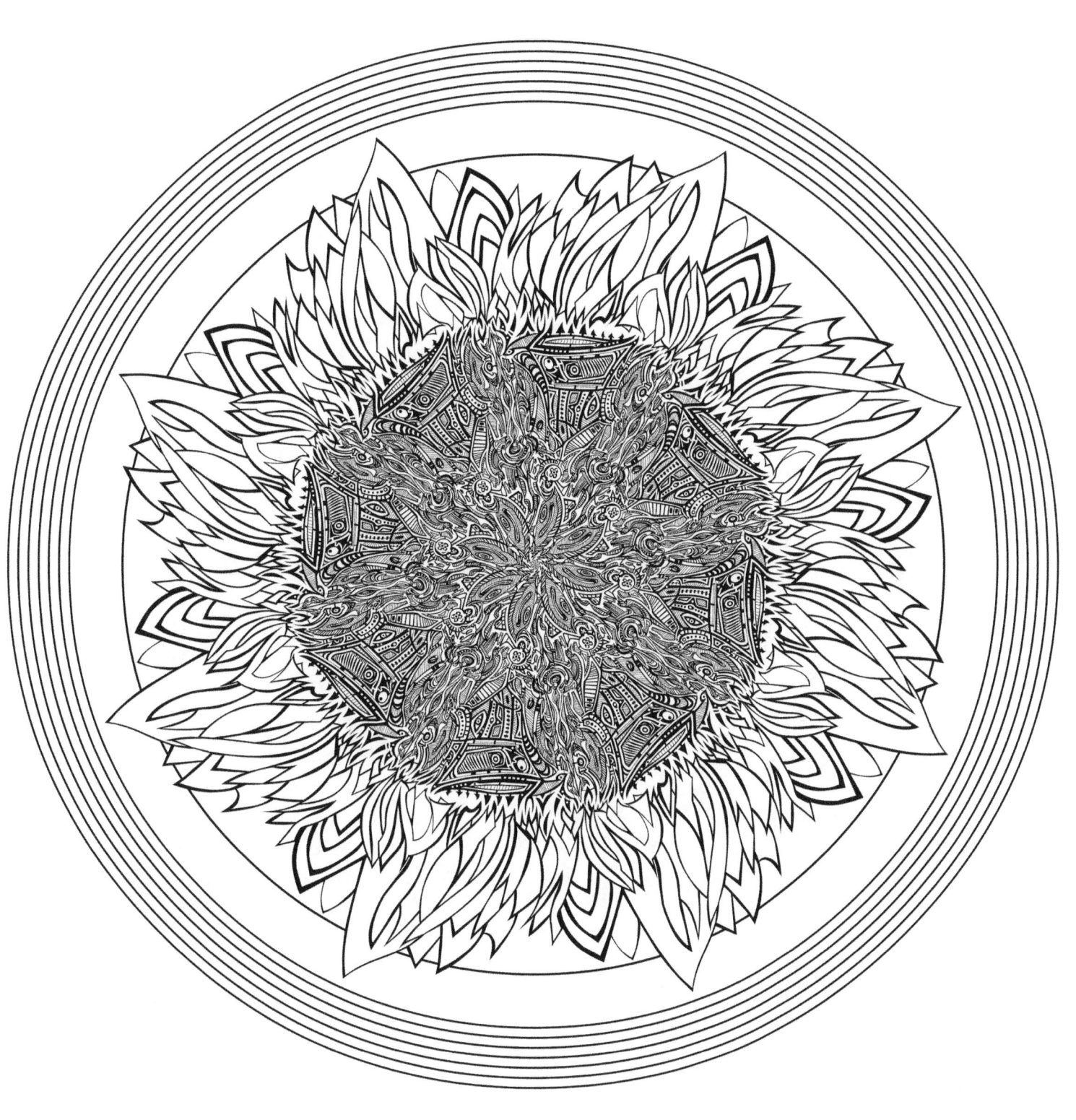

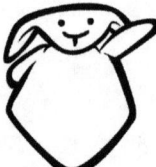

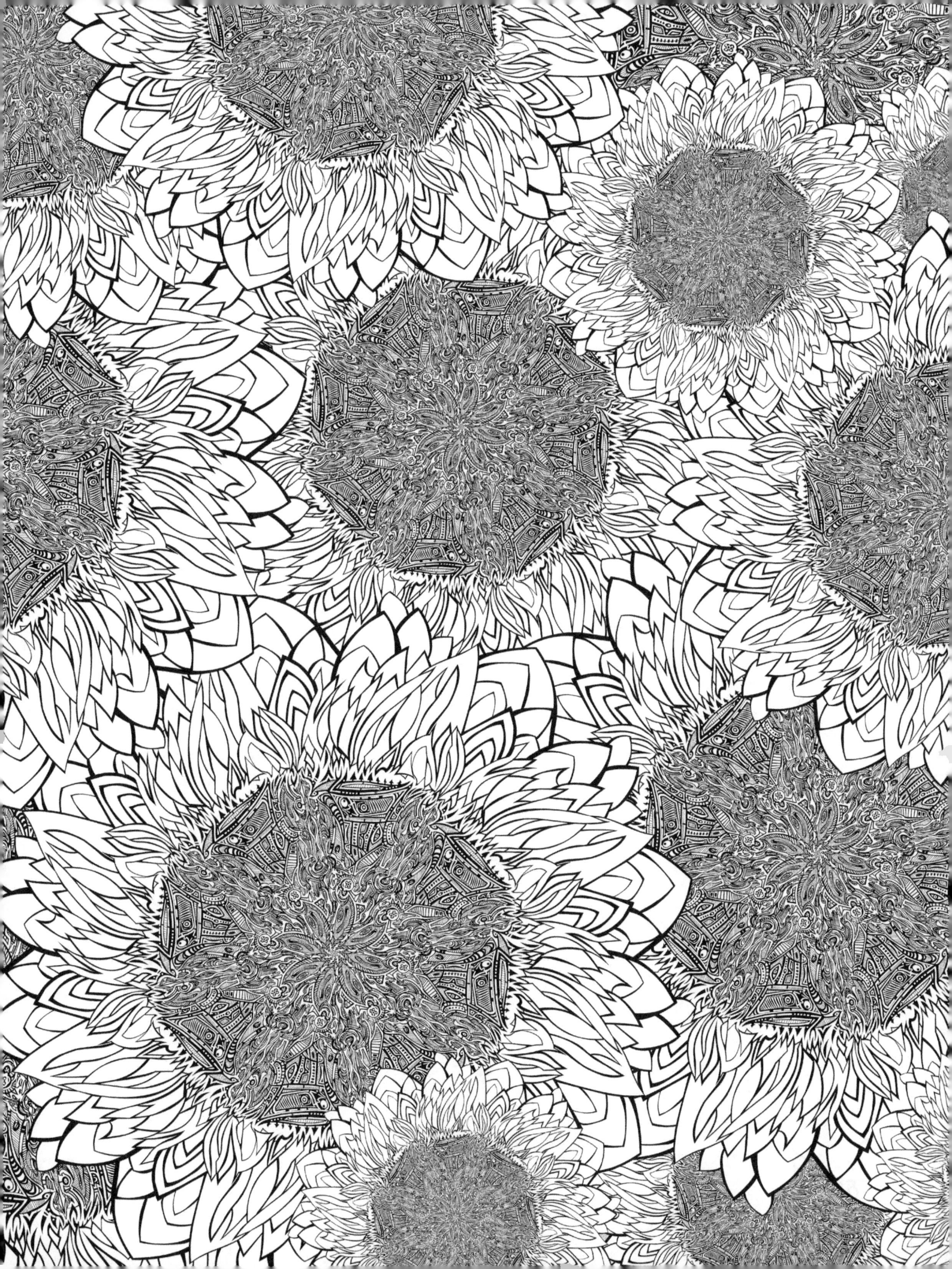

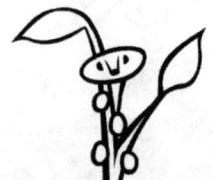

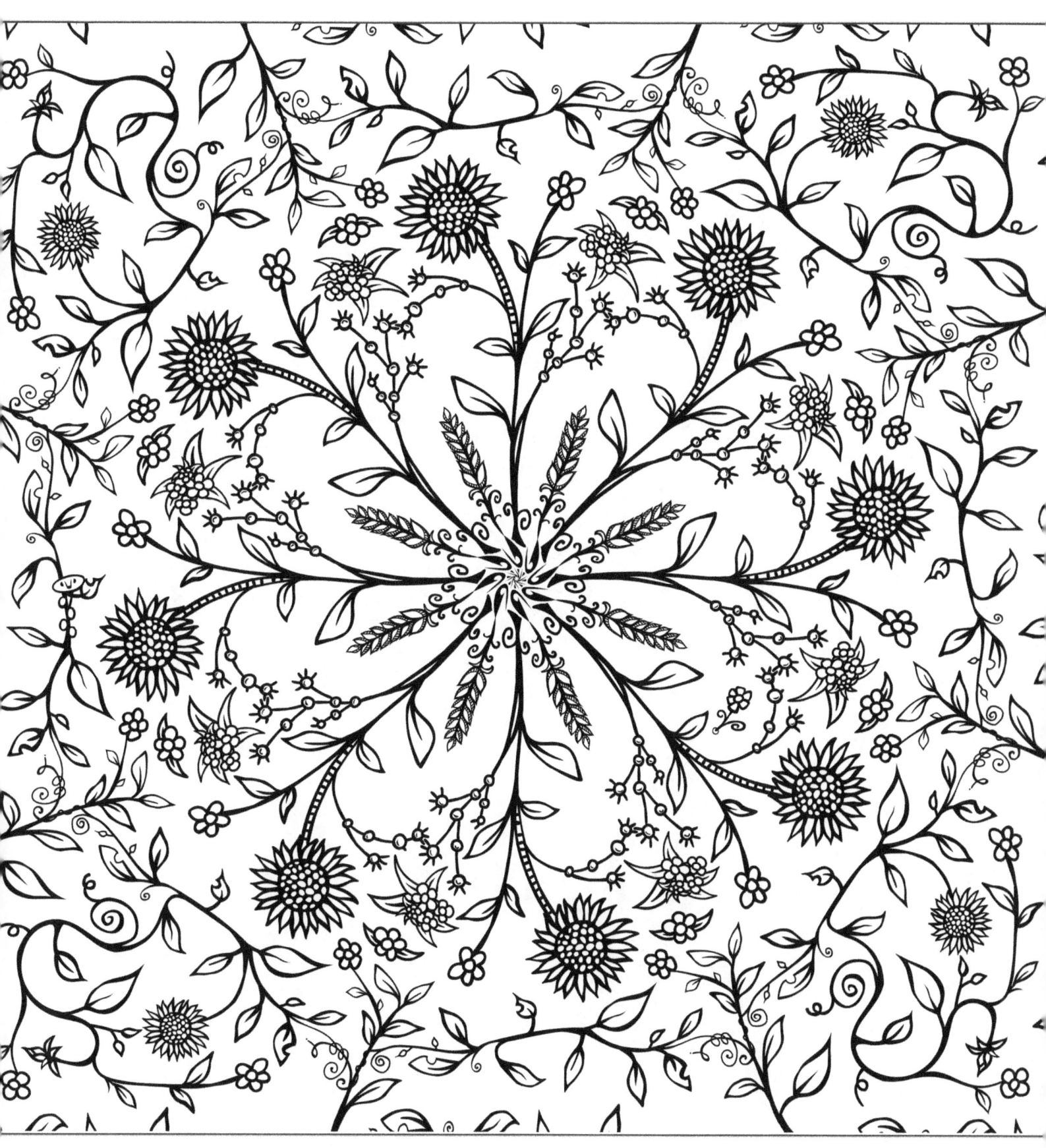

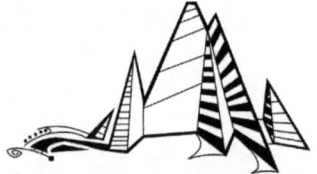

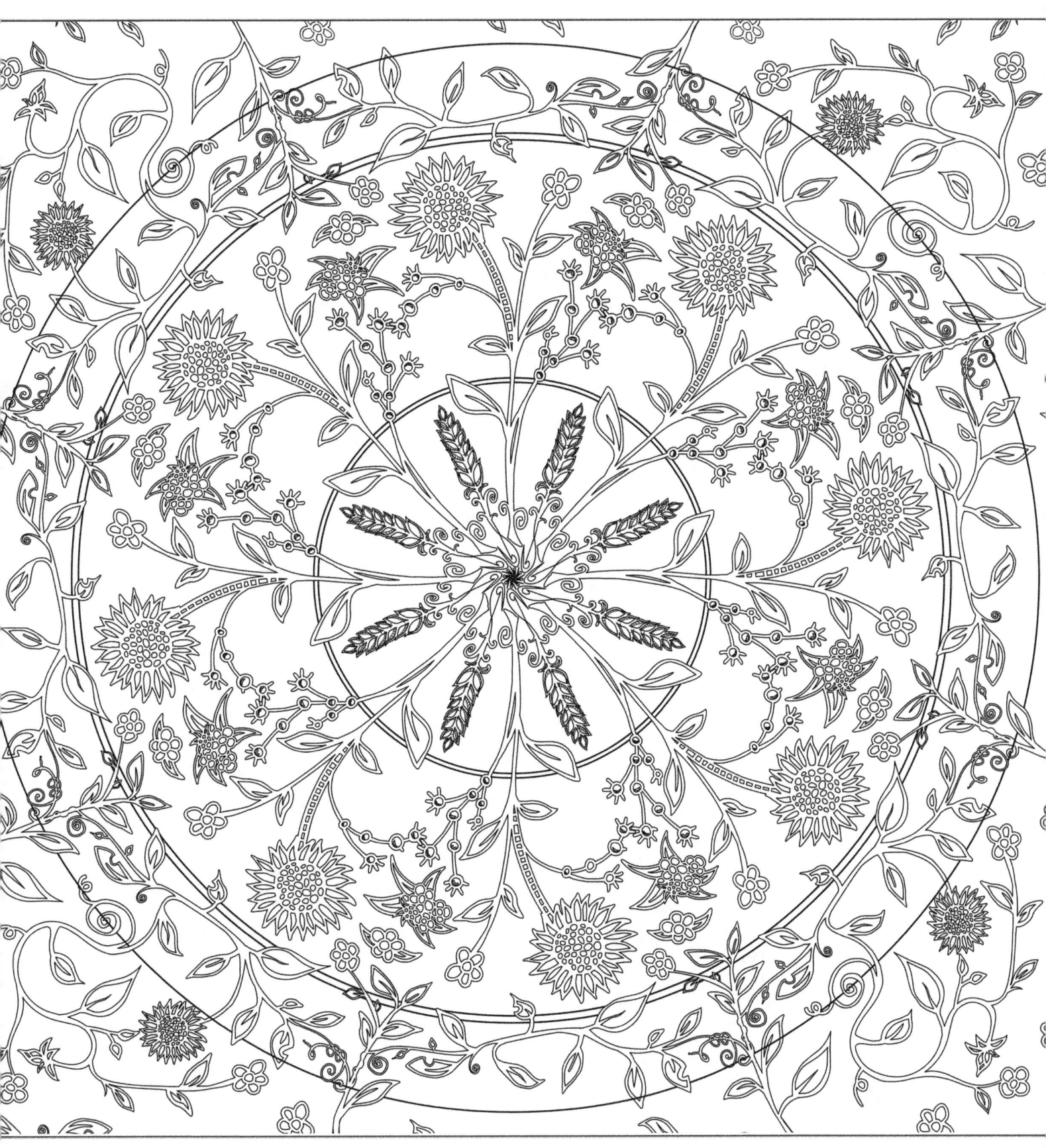

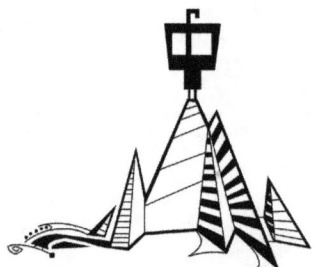

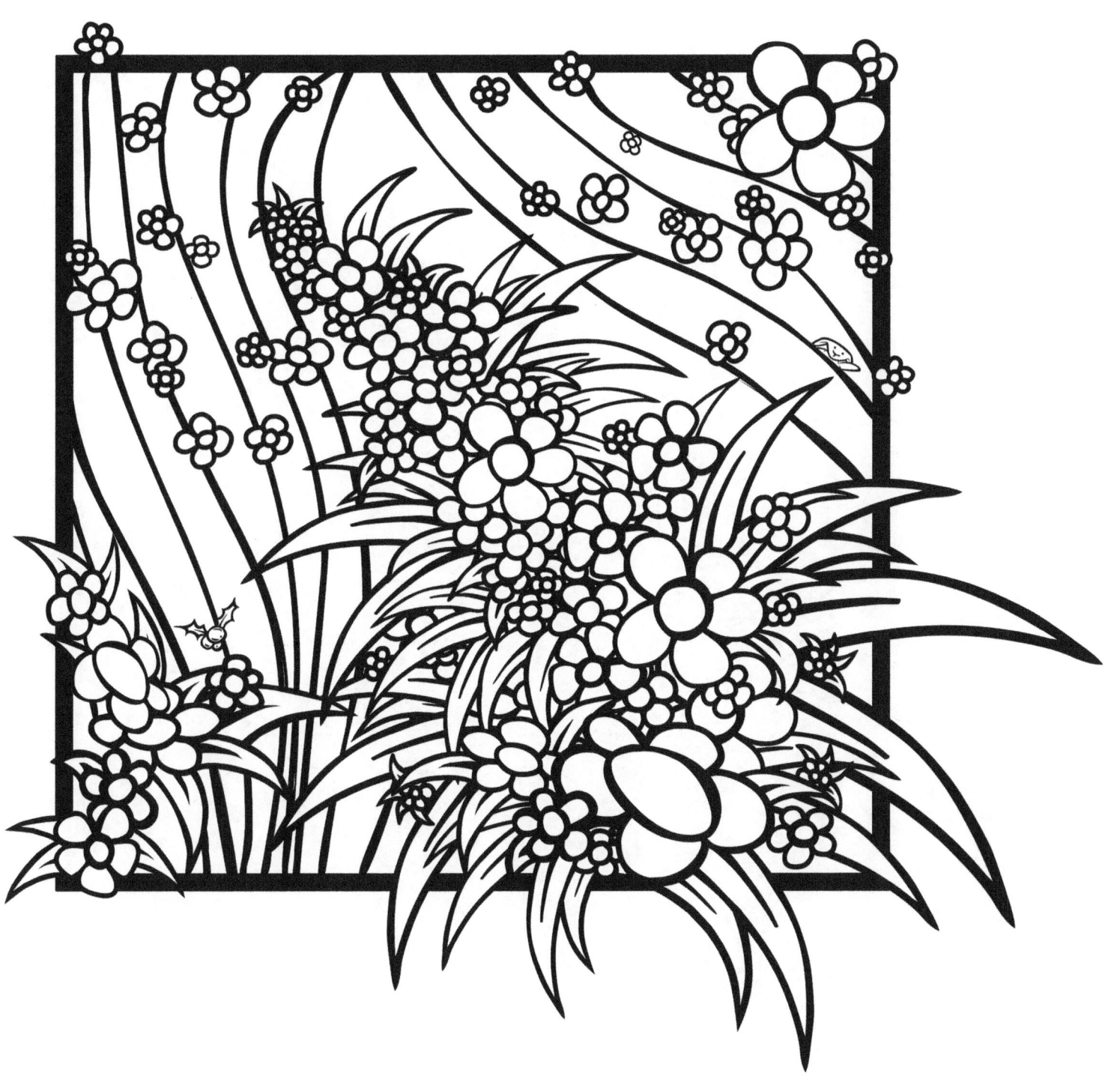

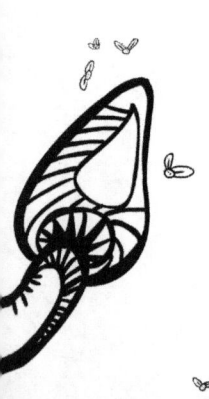

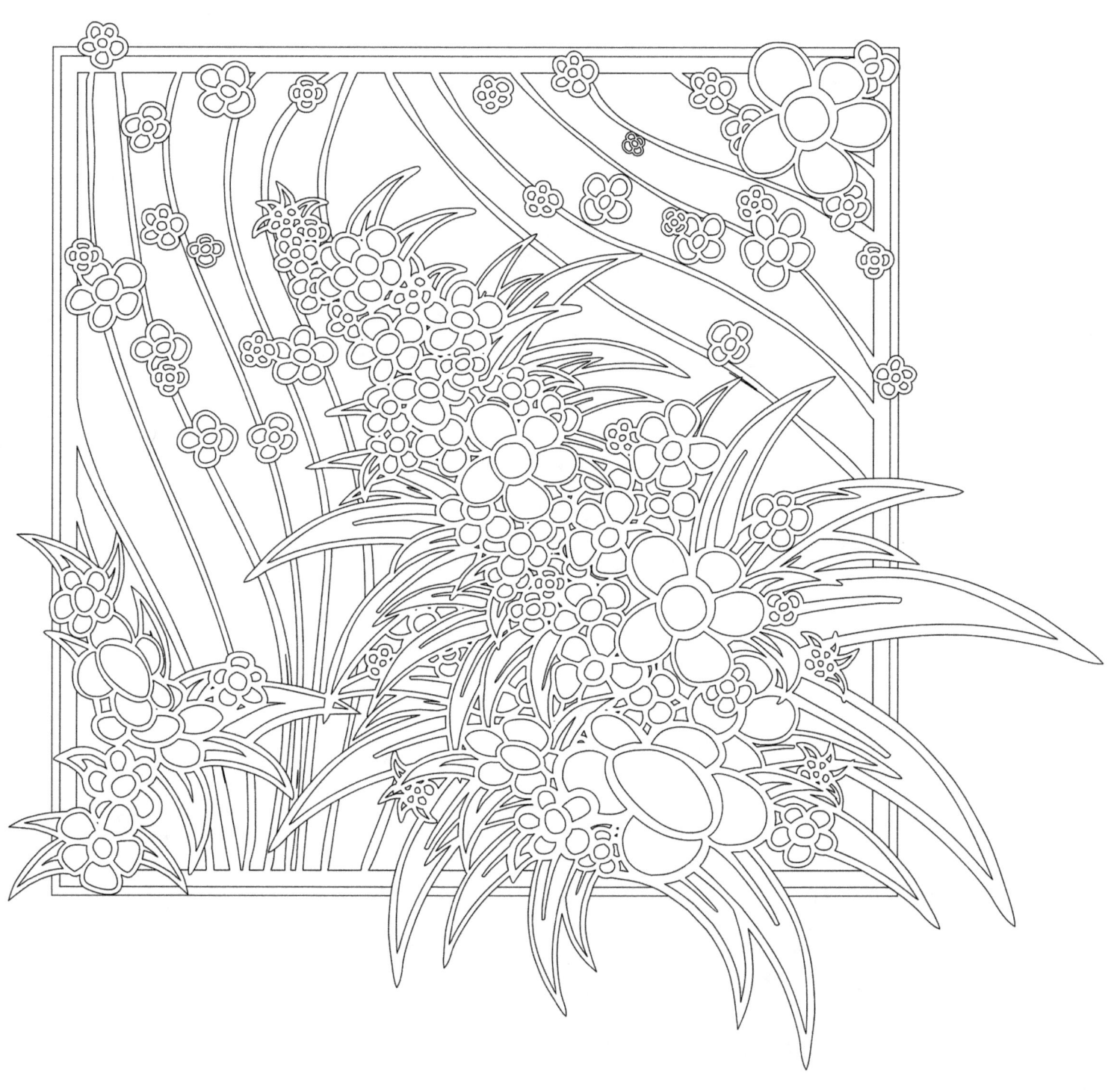

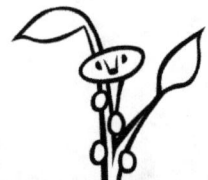

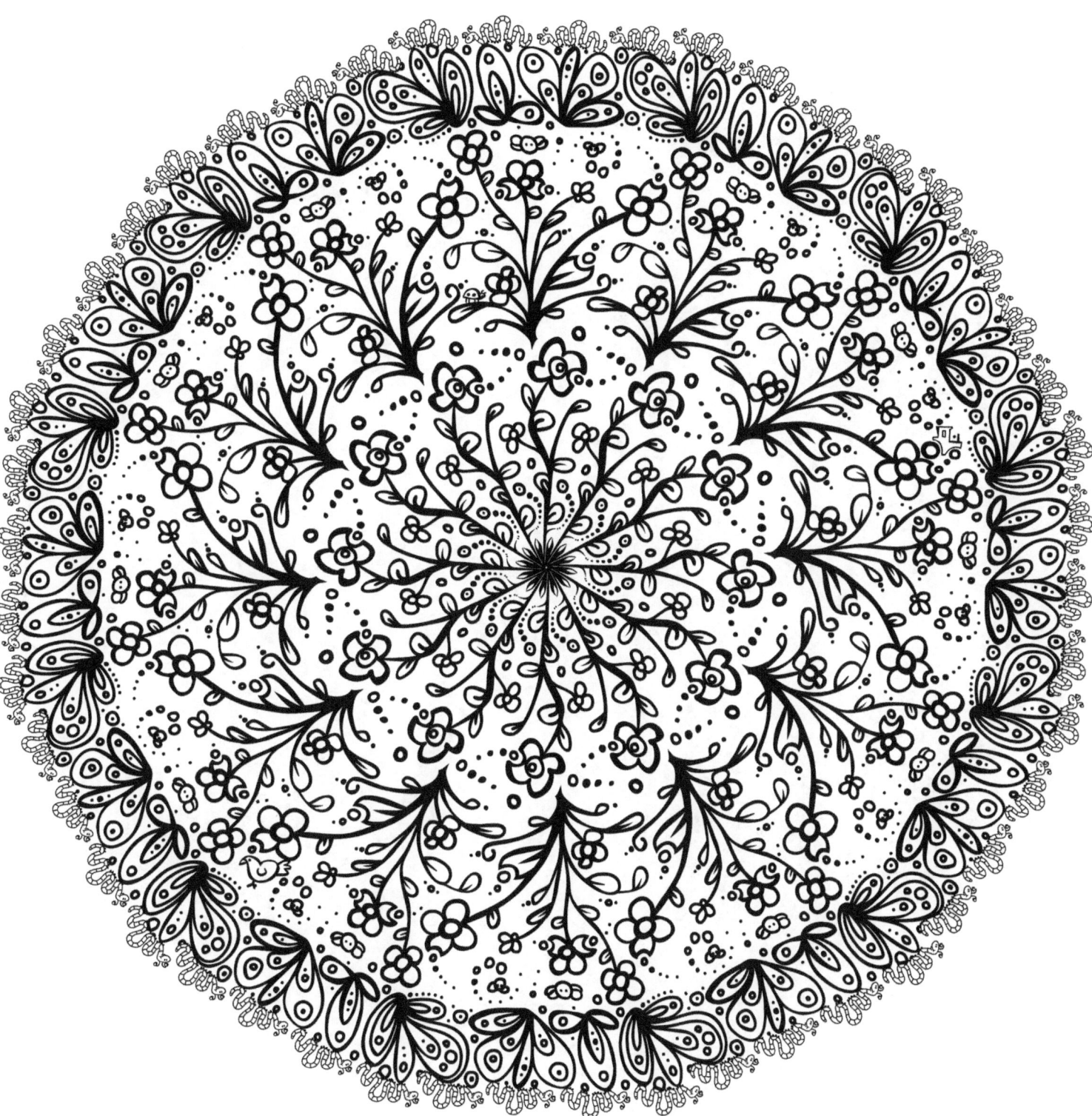

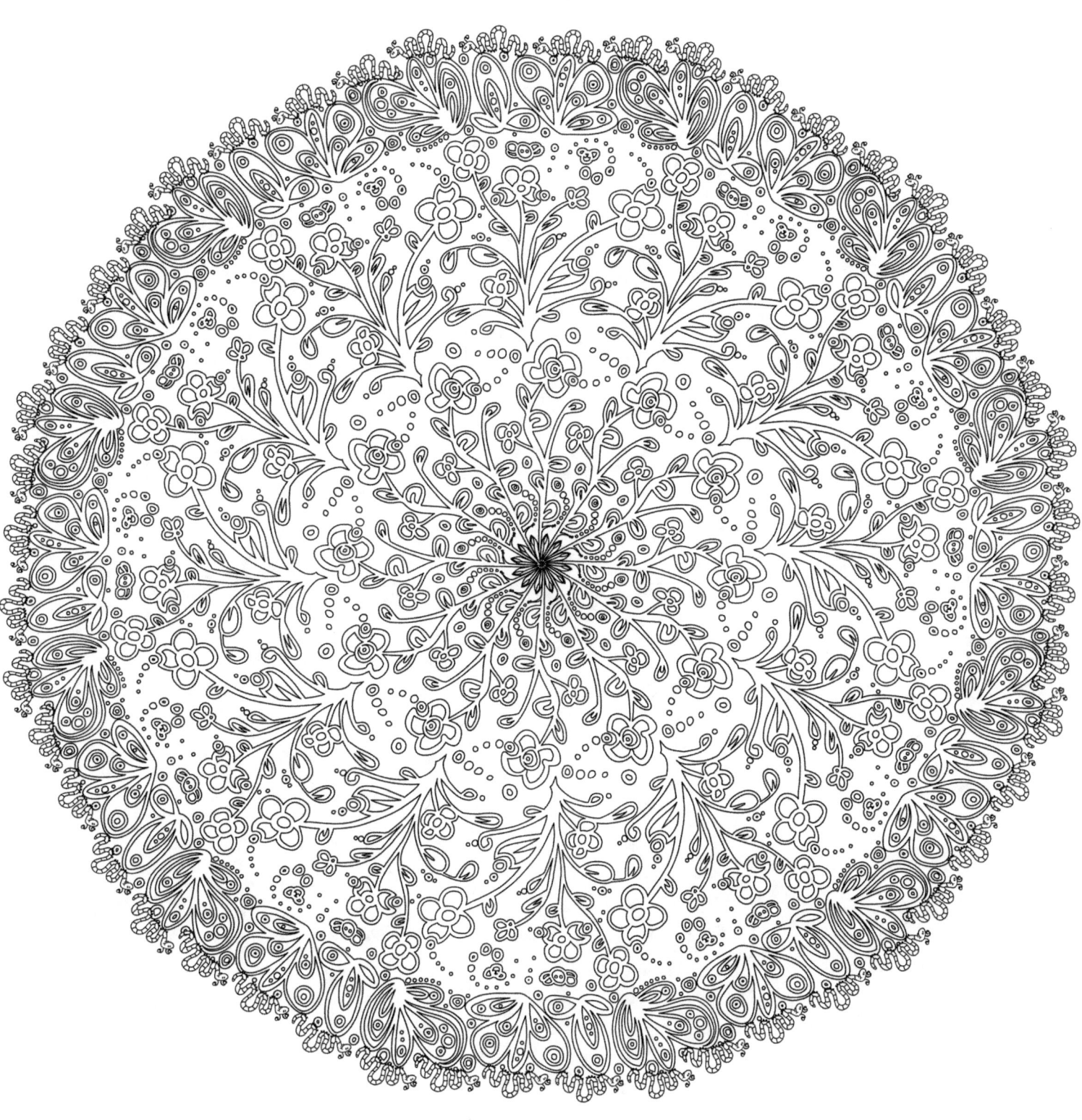

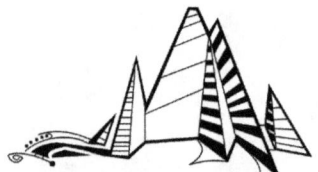

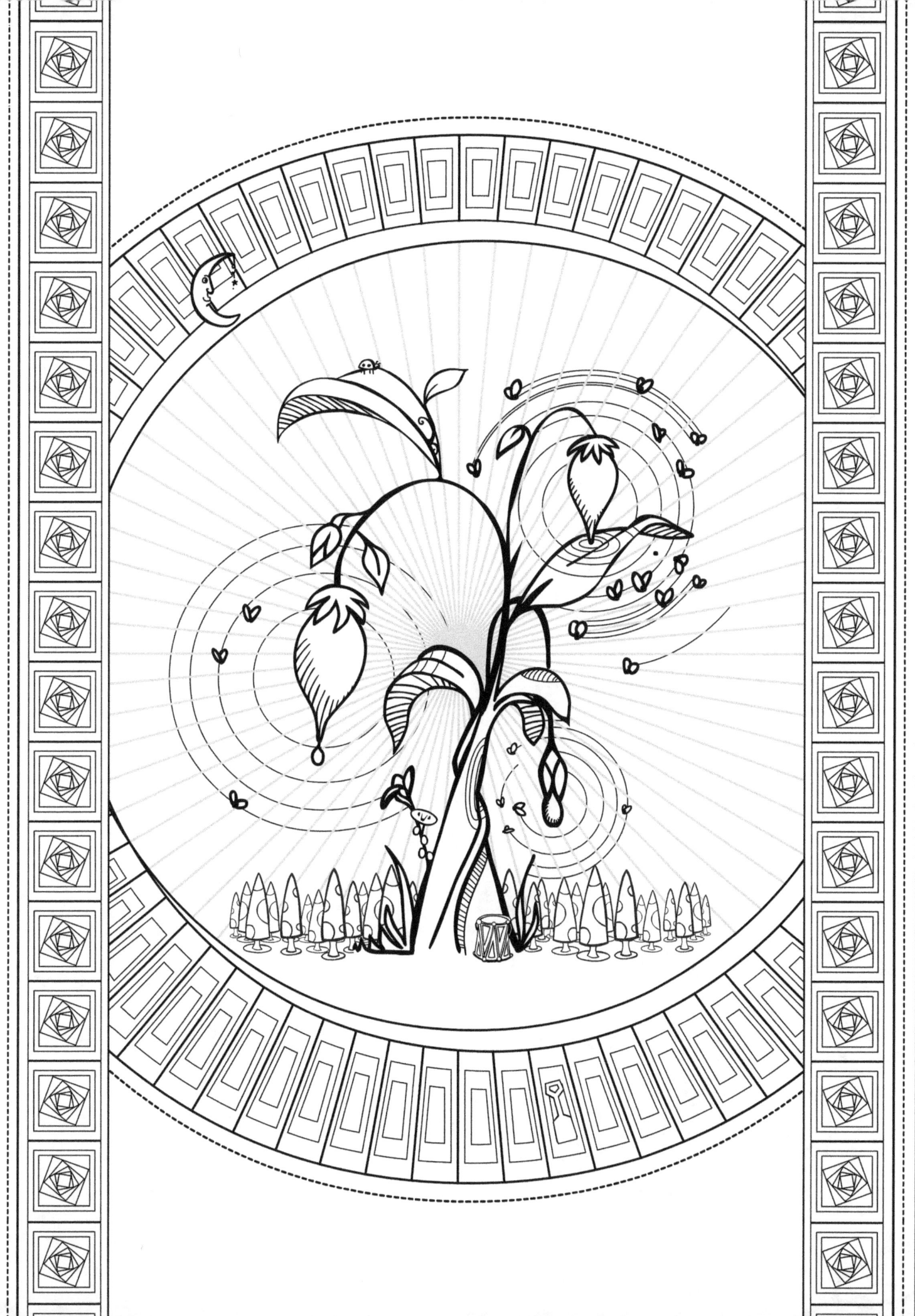

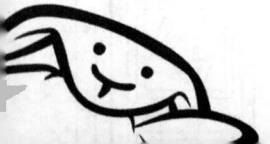

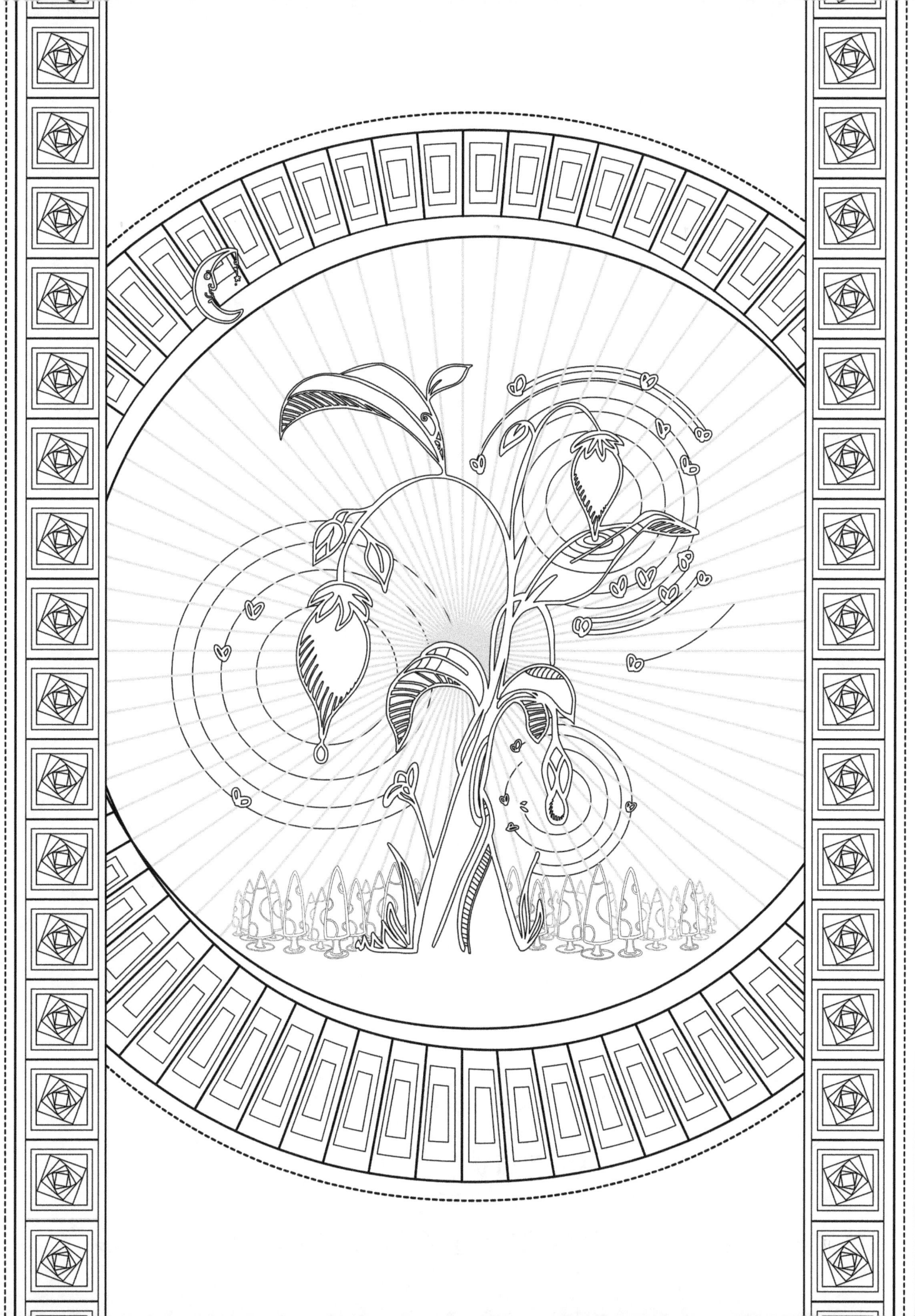

PART FIVE

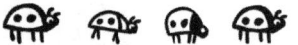 GENERALLY ABSTRACTED   >>

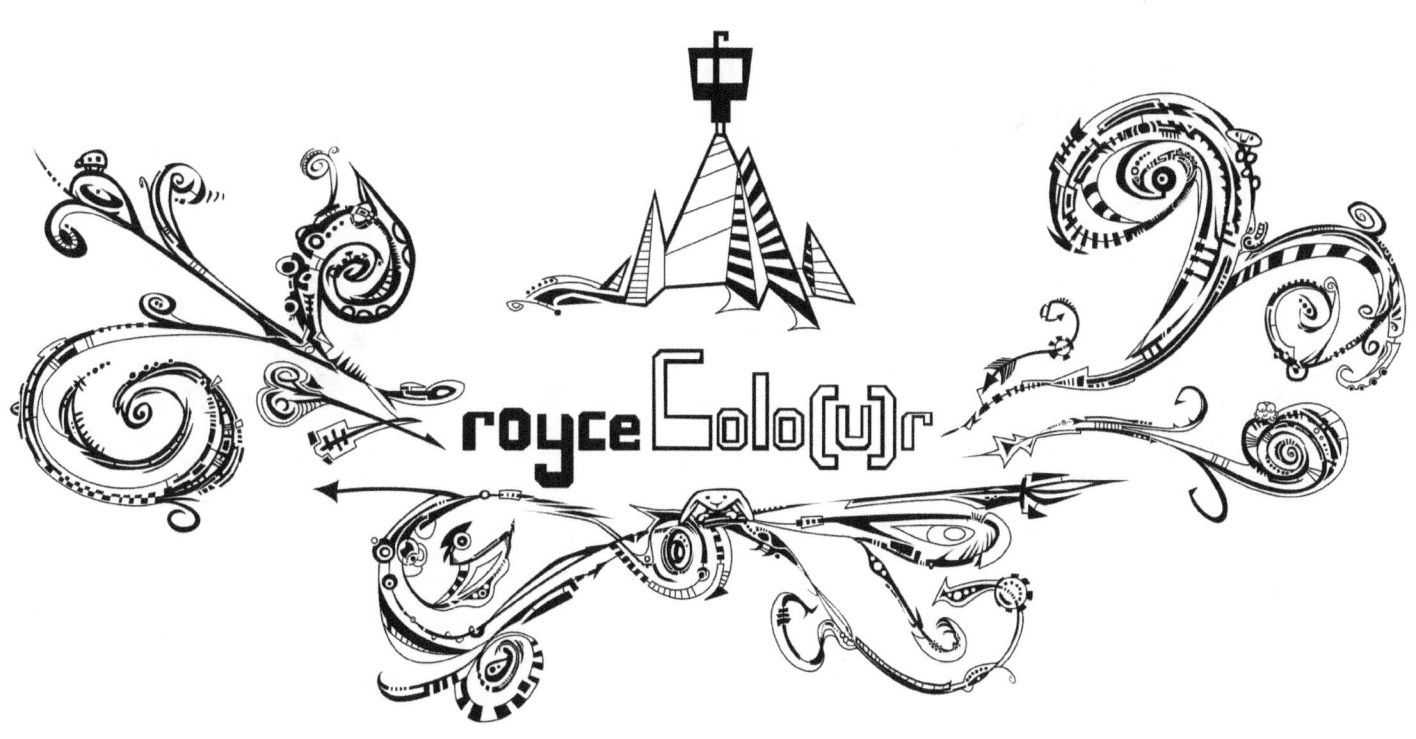

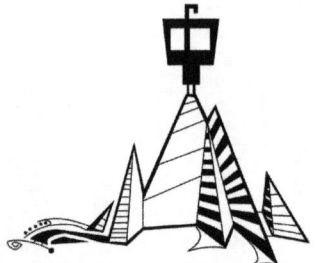

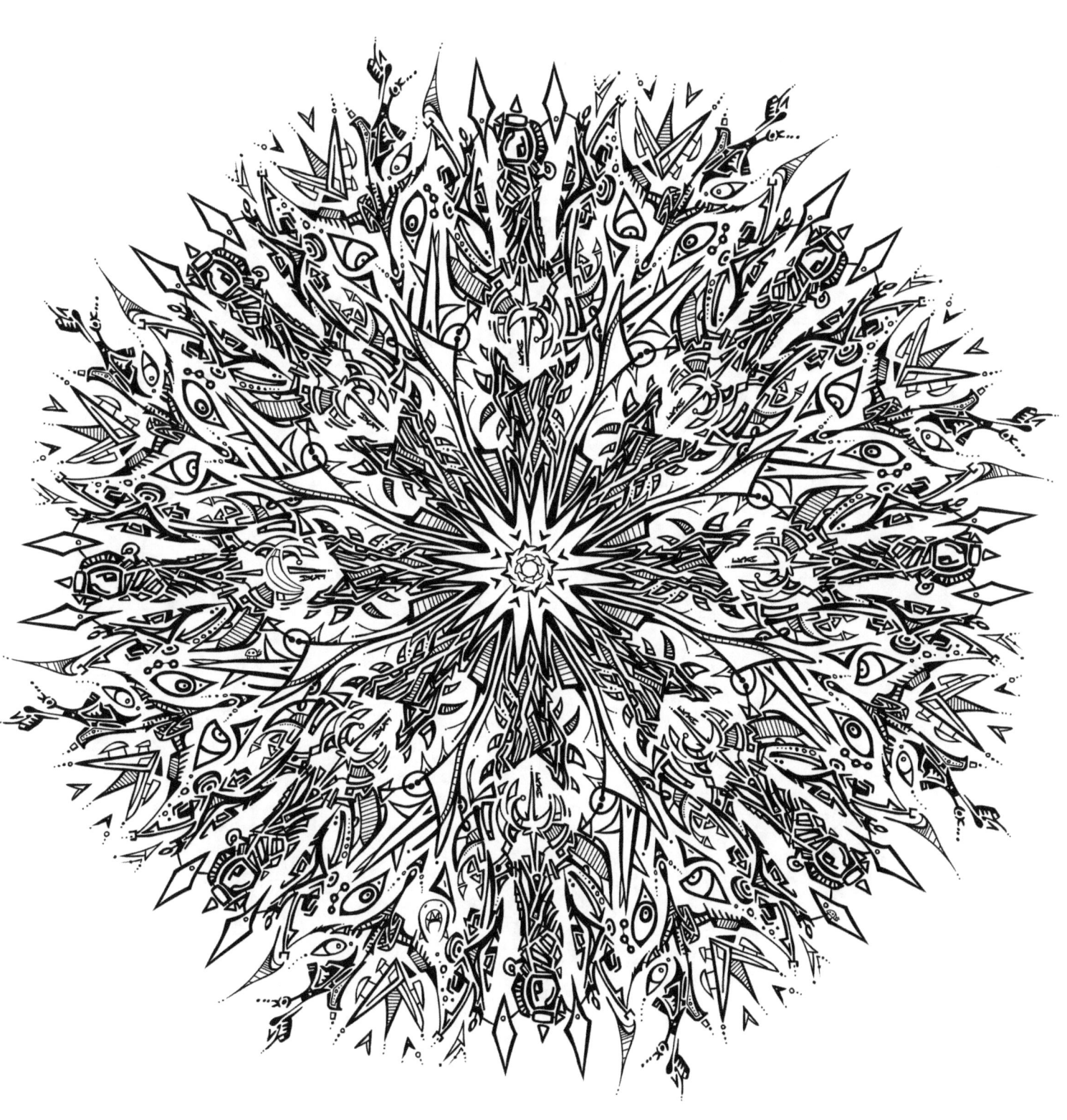

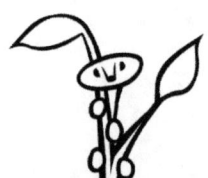

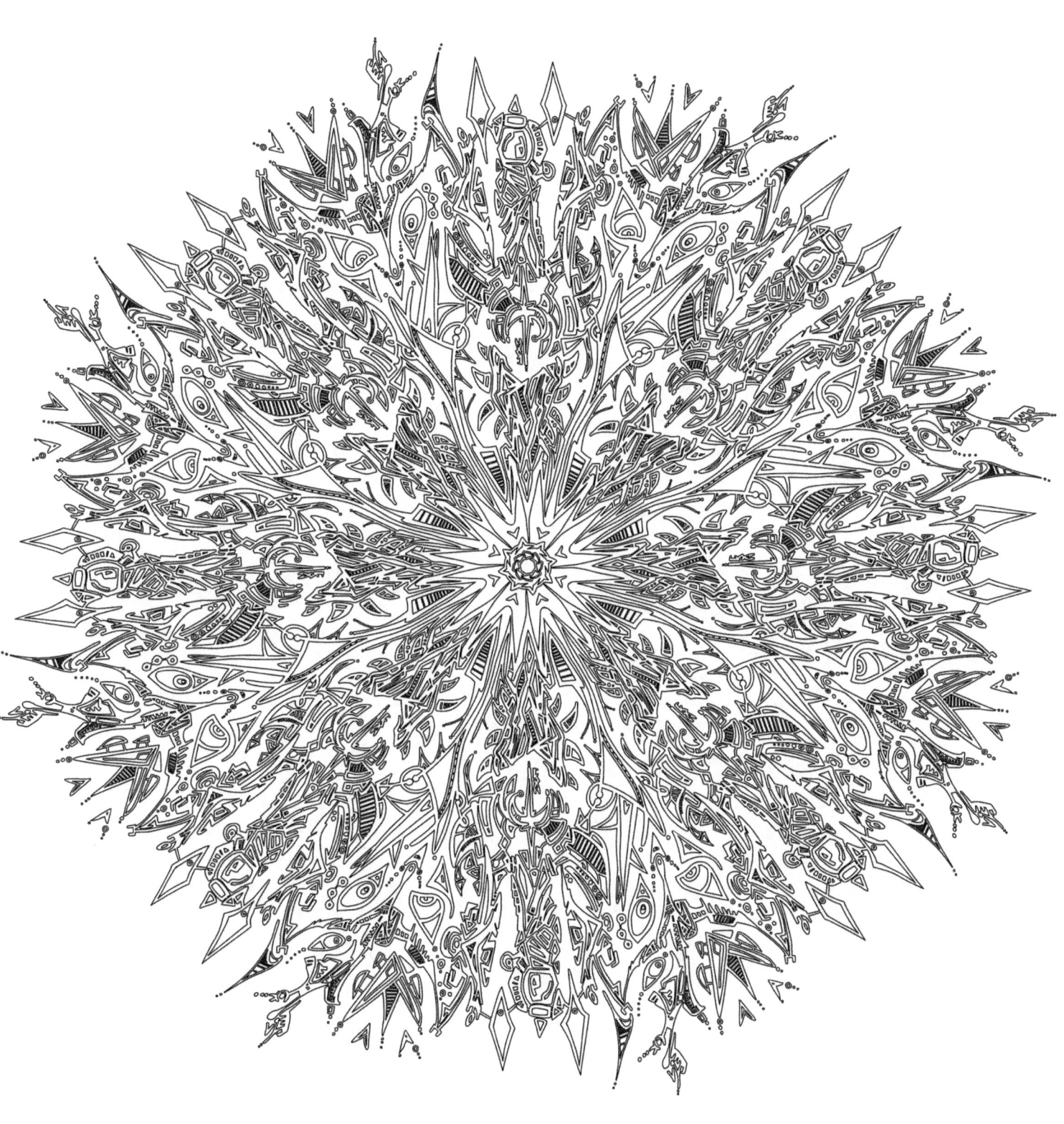

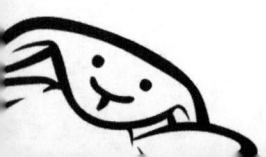

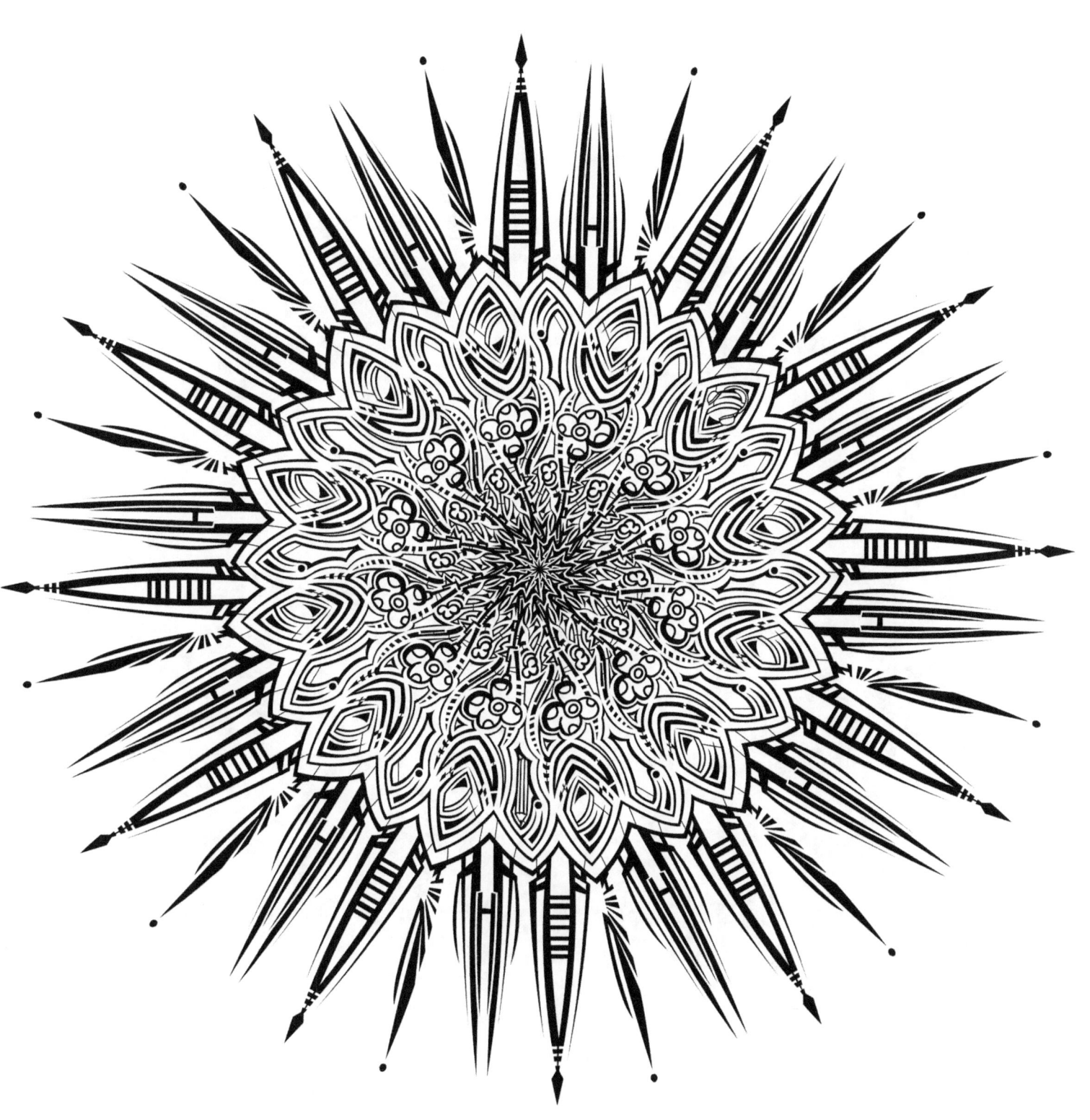

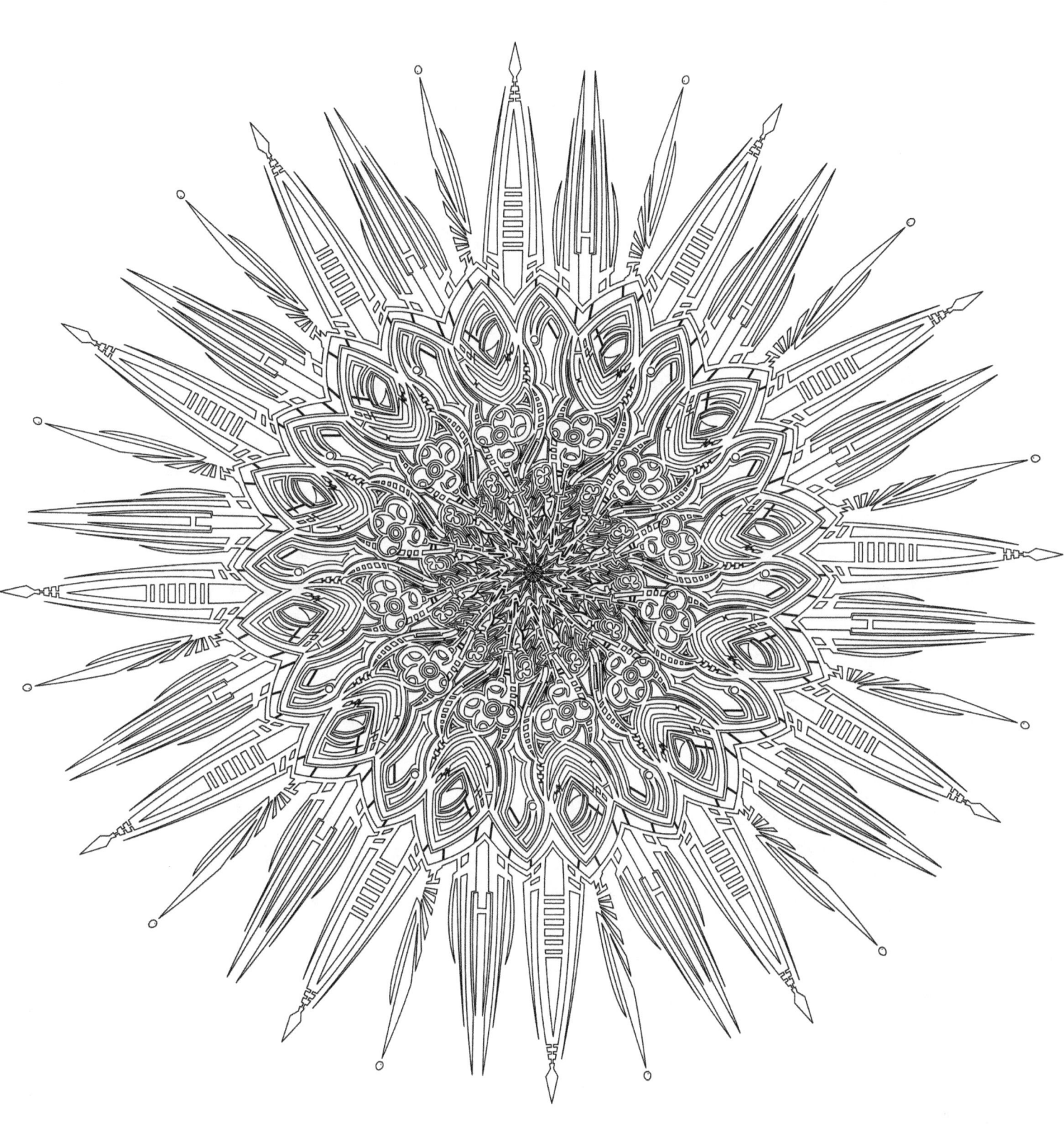

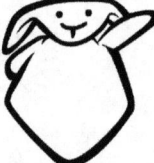

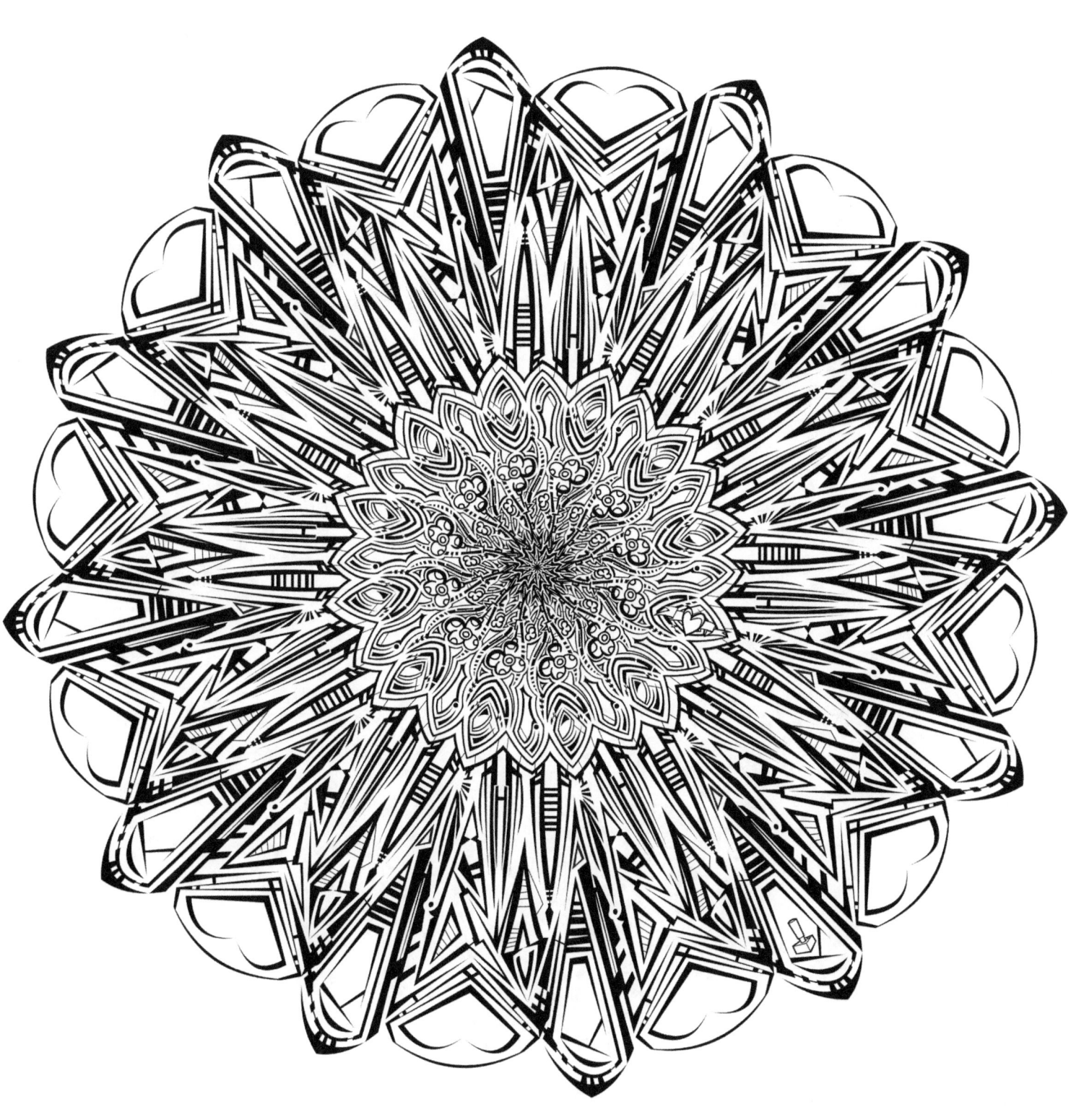

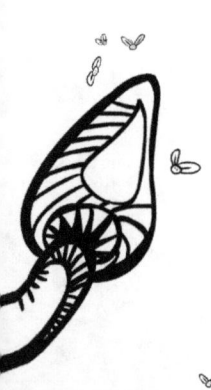

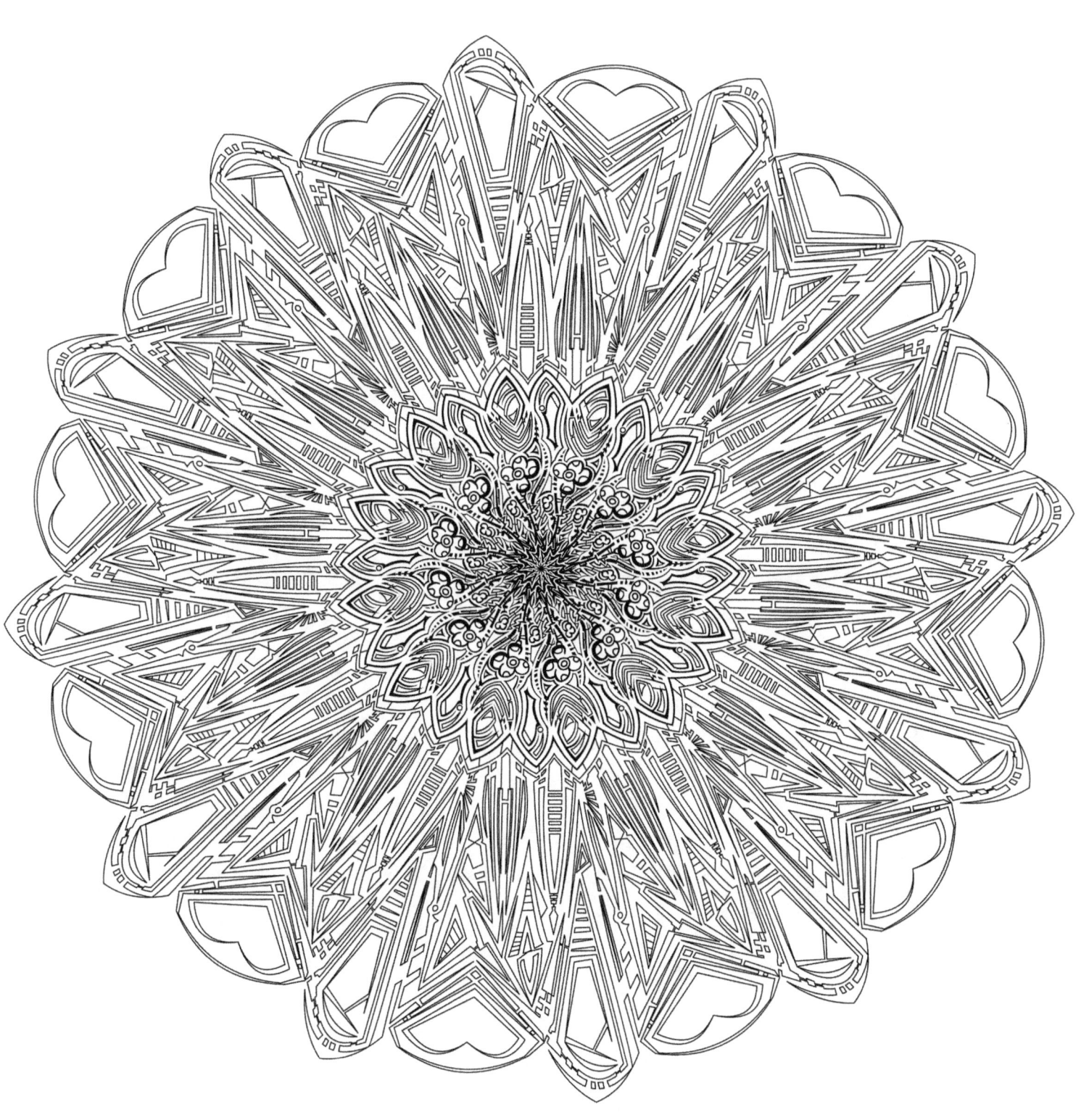

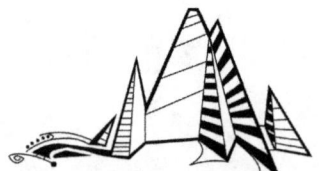

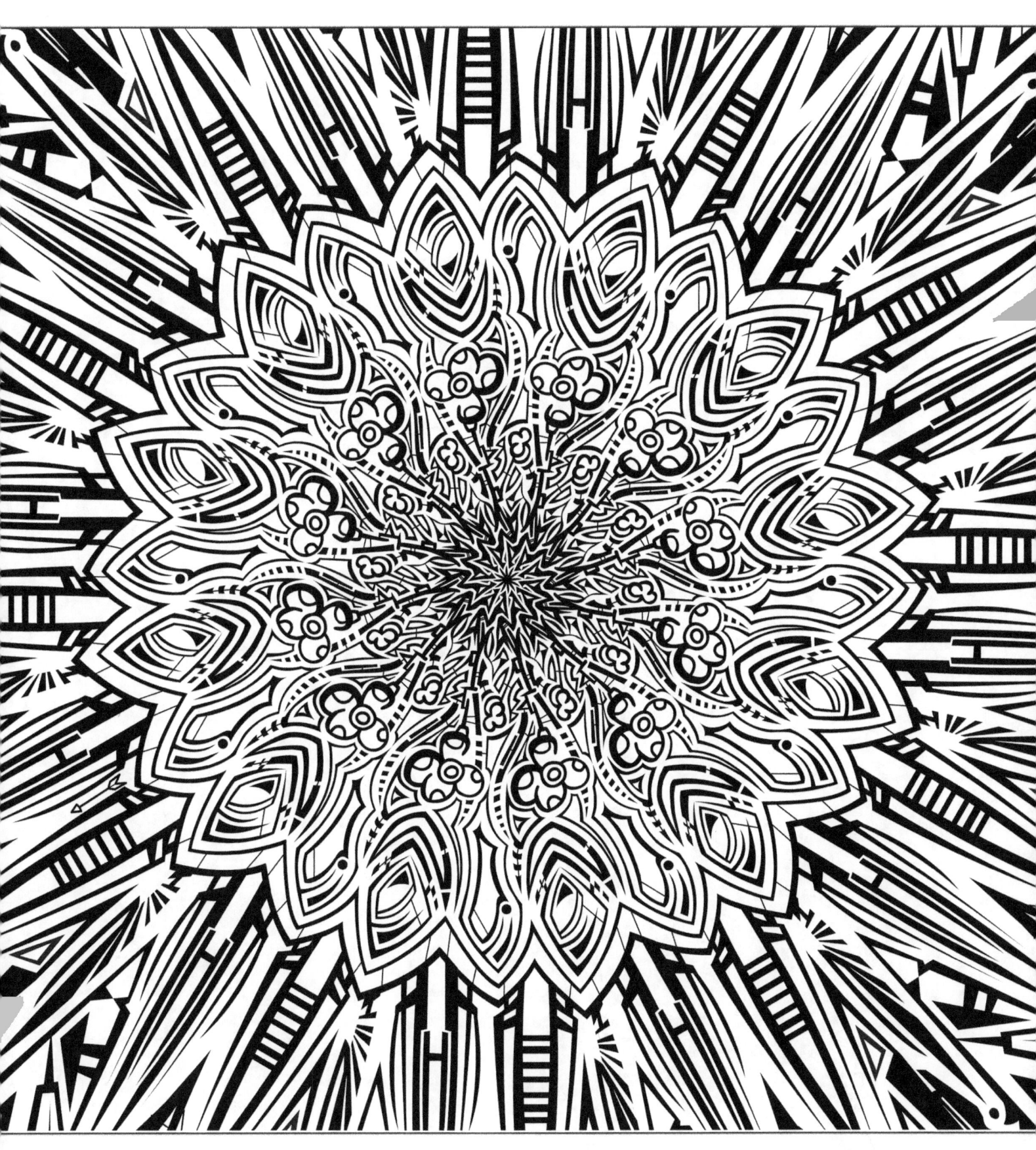

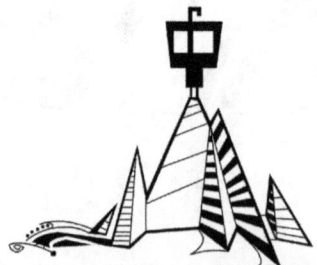

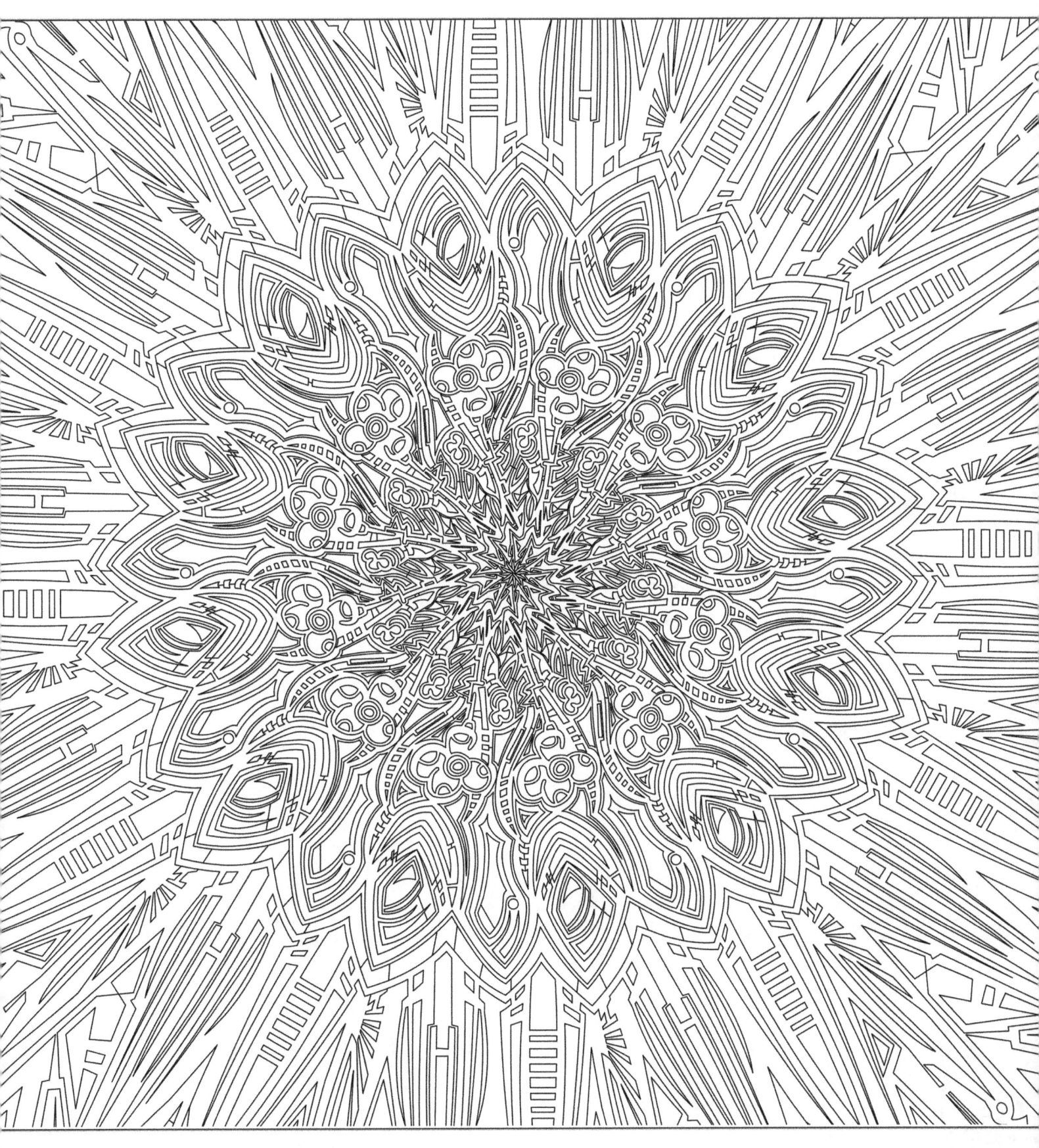

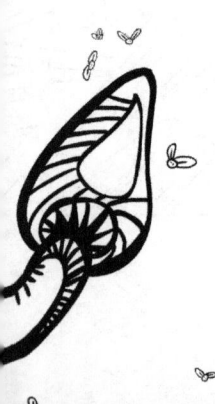

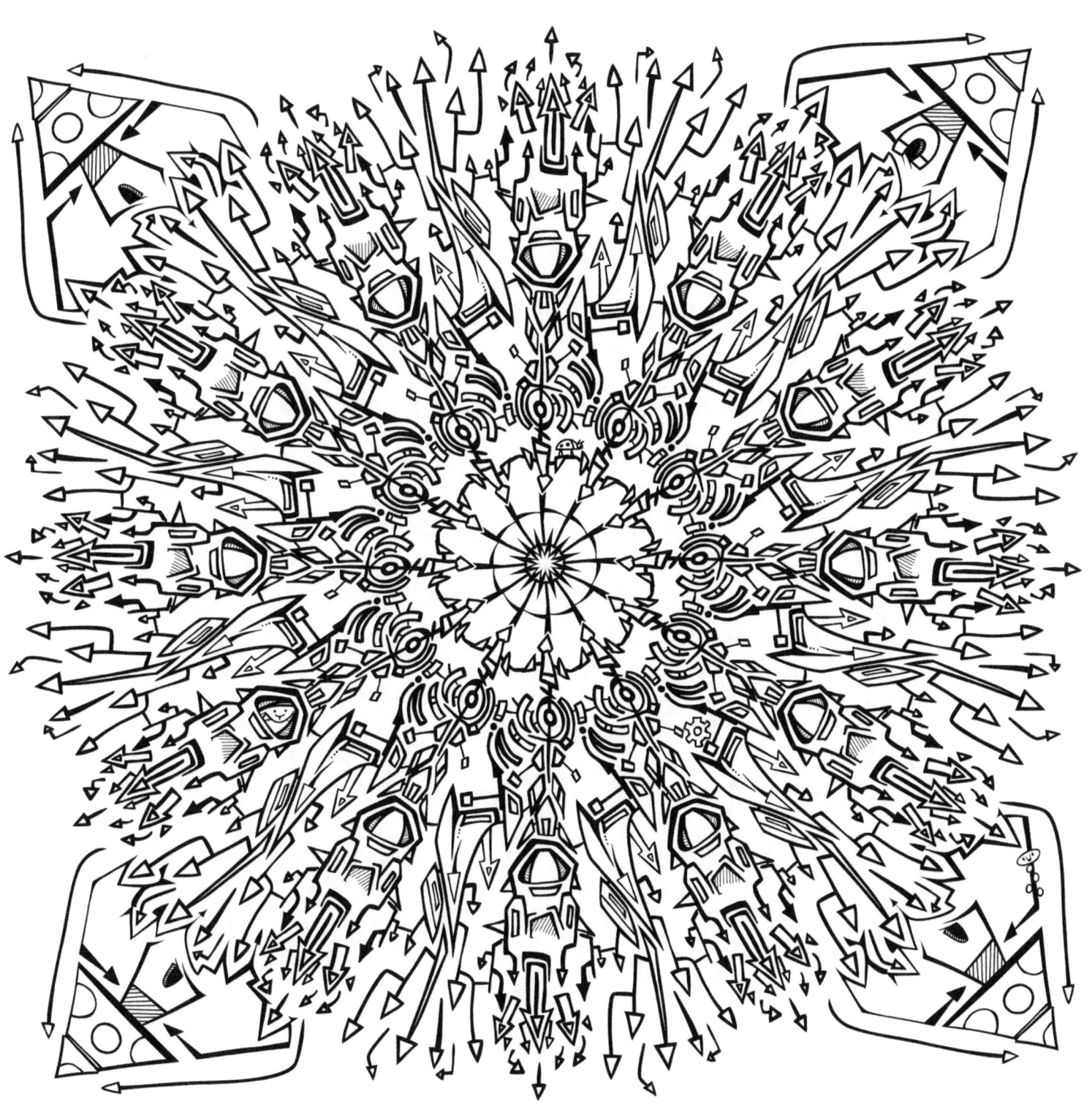

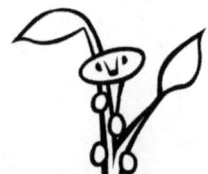

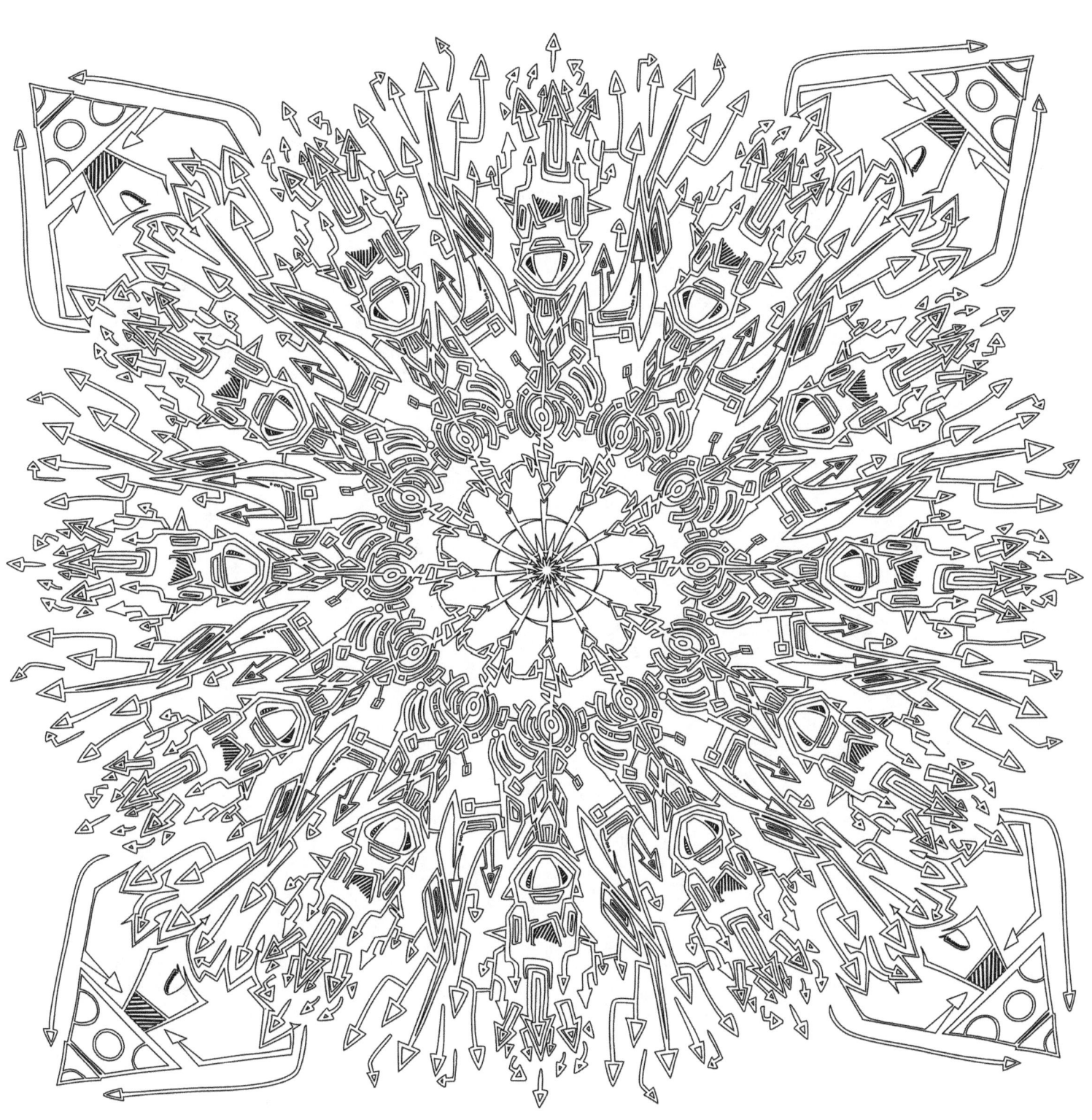

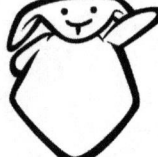

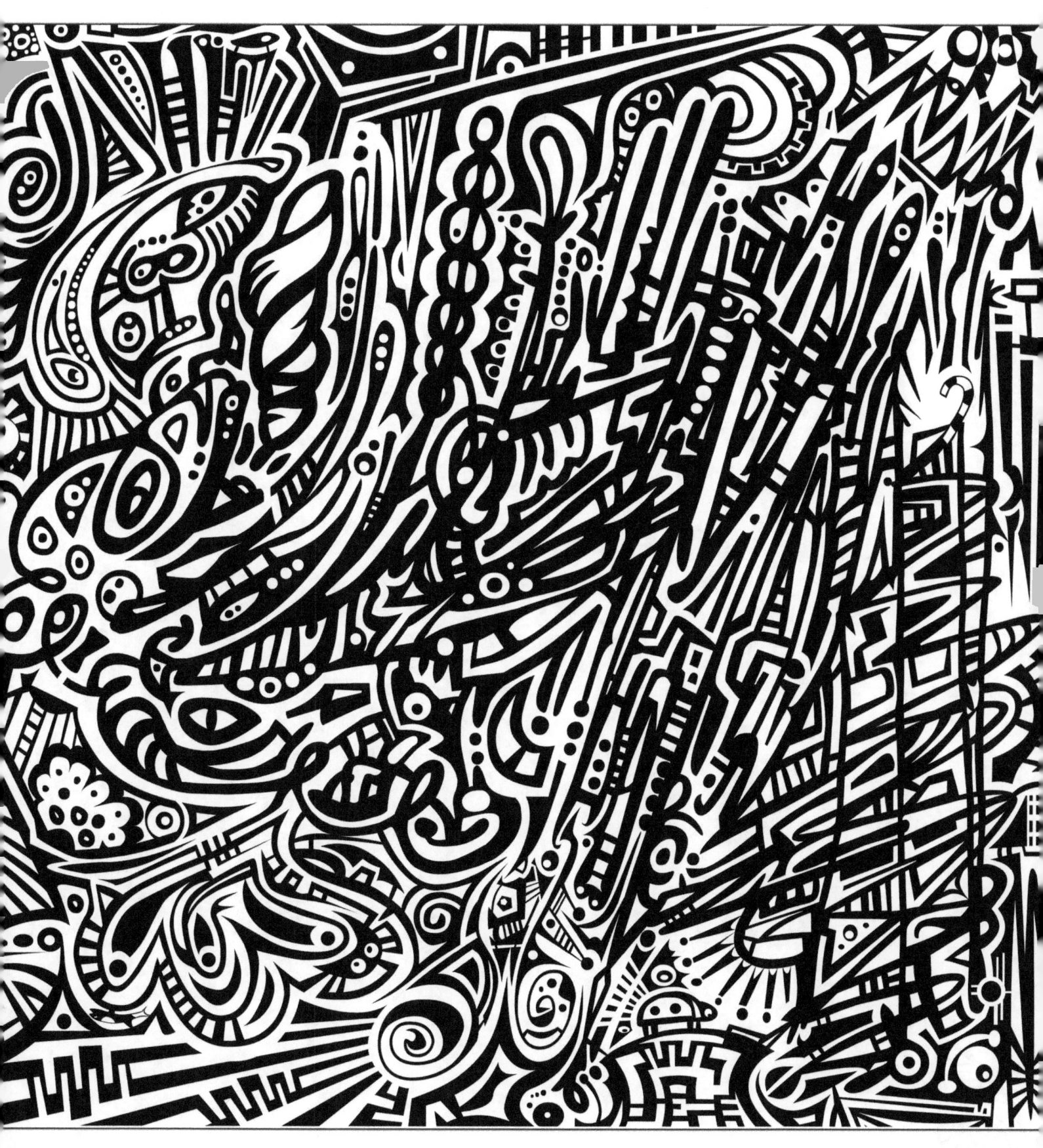

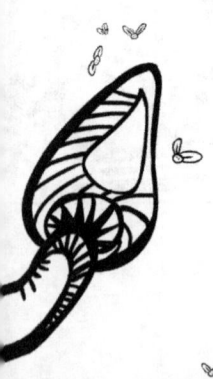

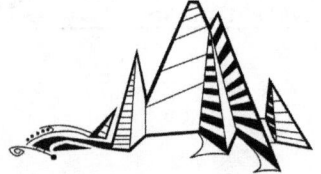

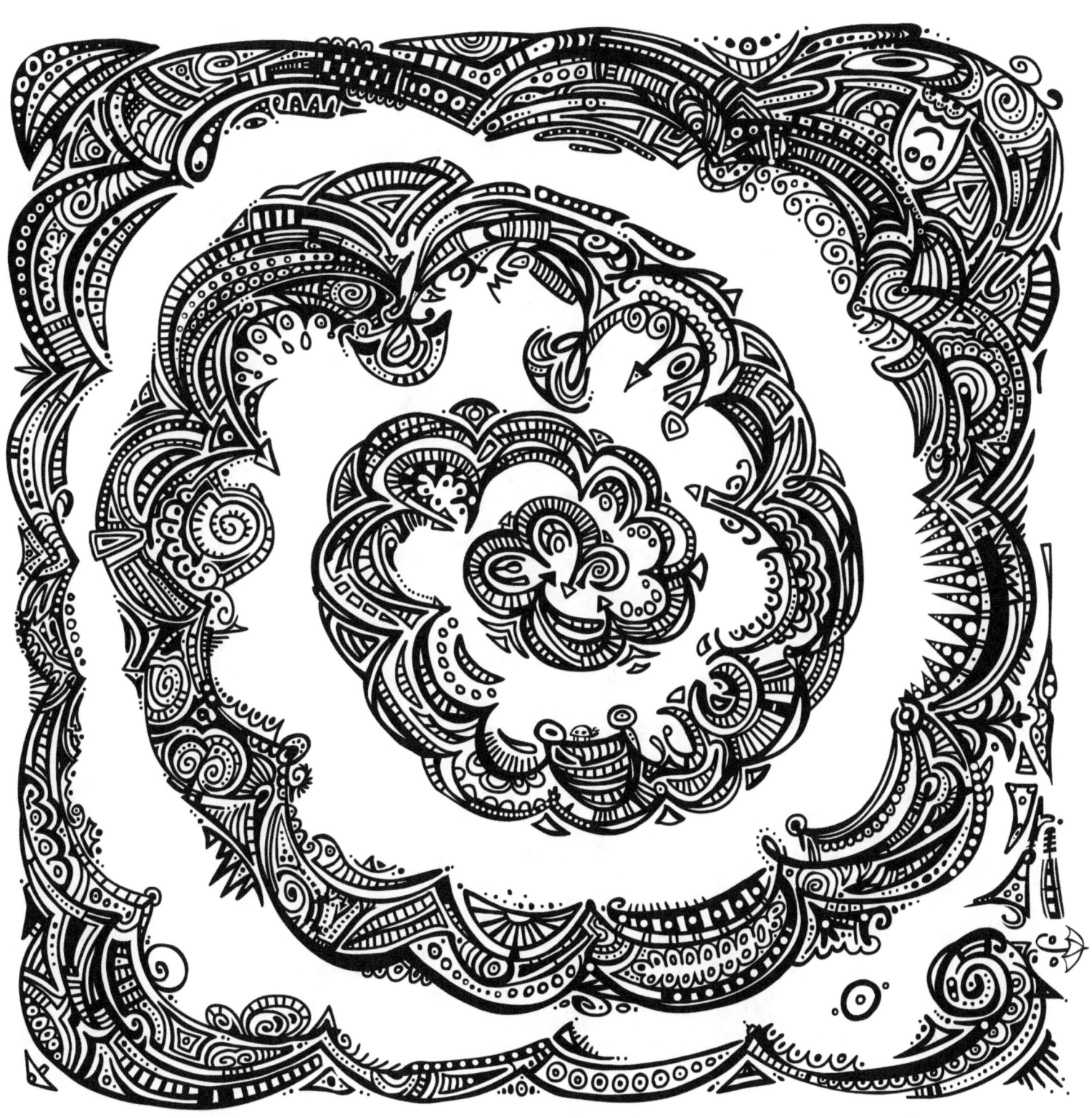

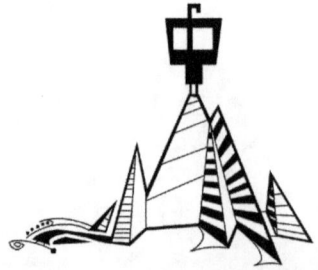

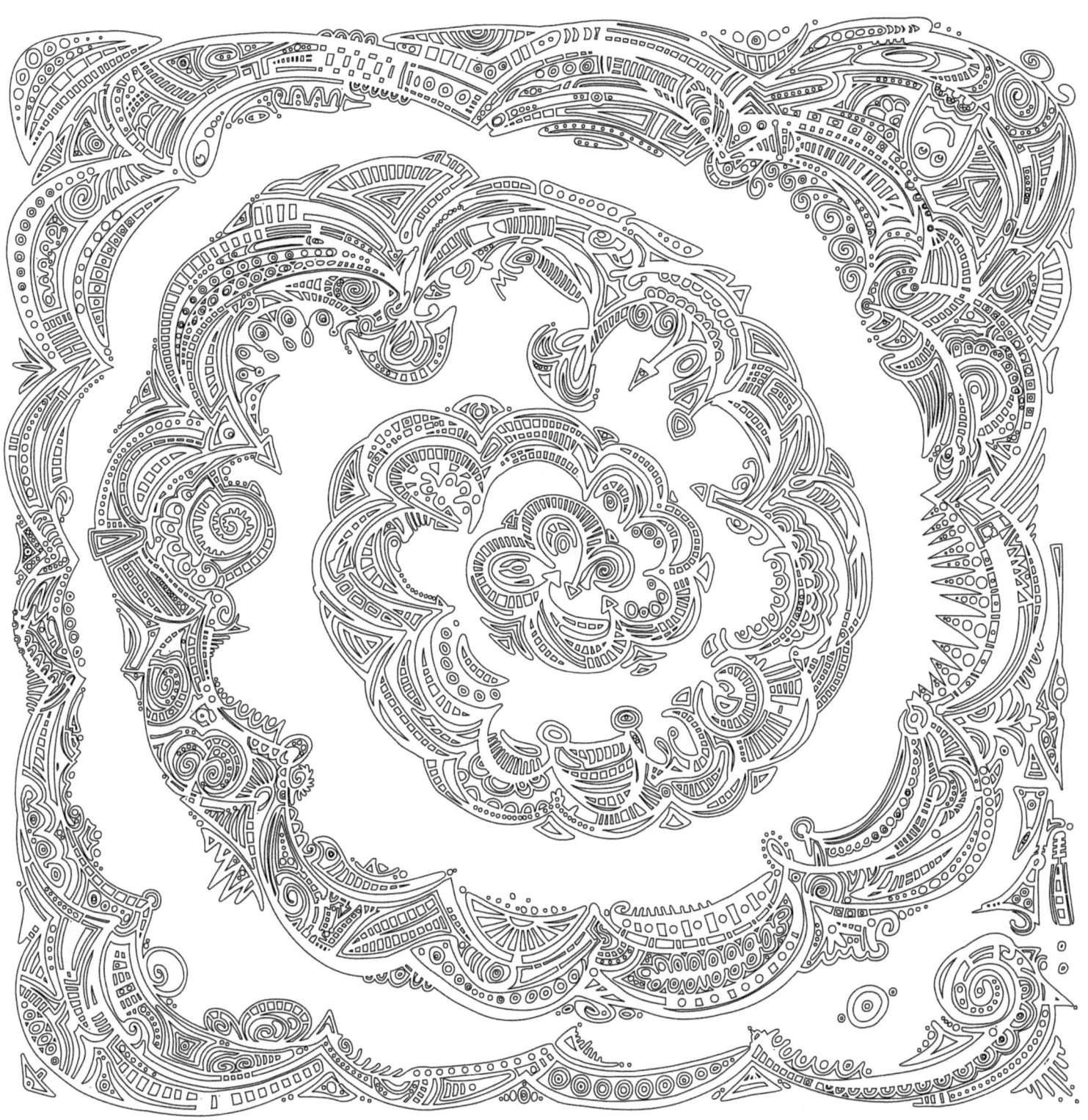

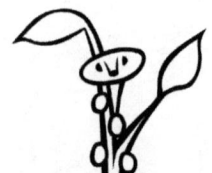

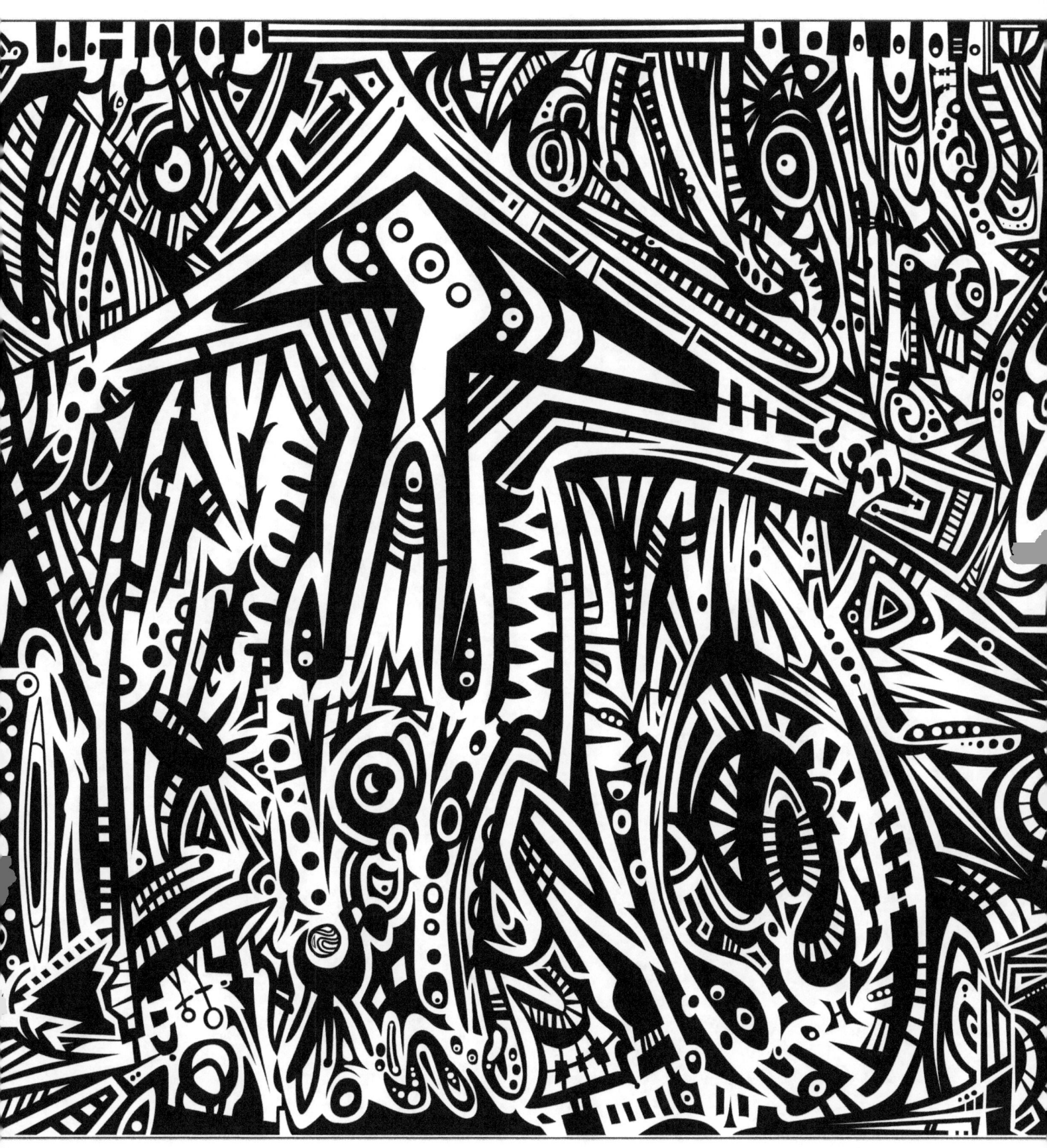

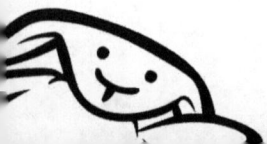

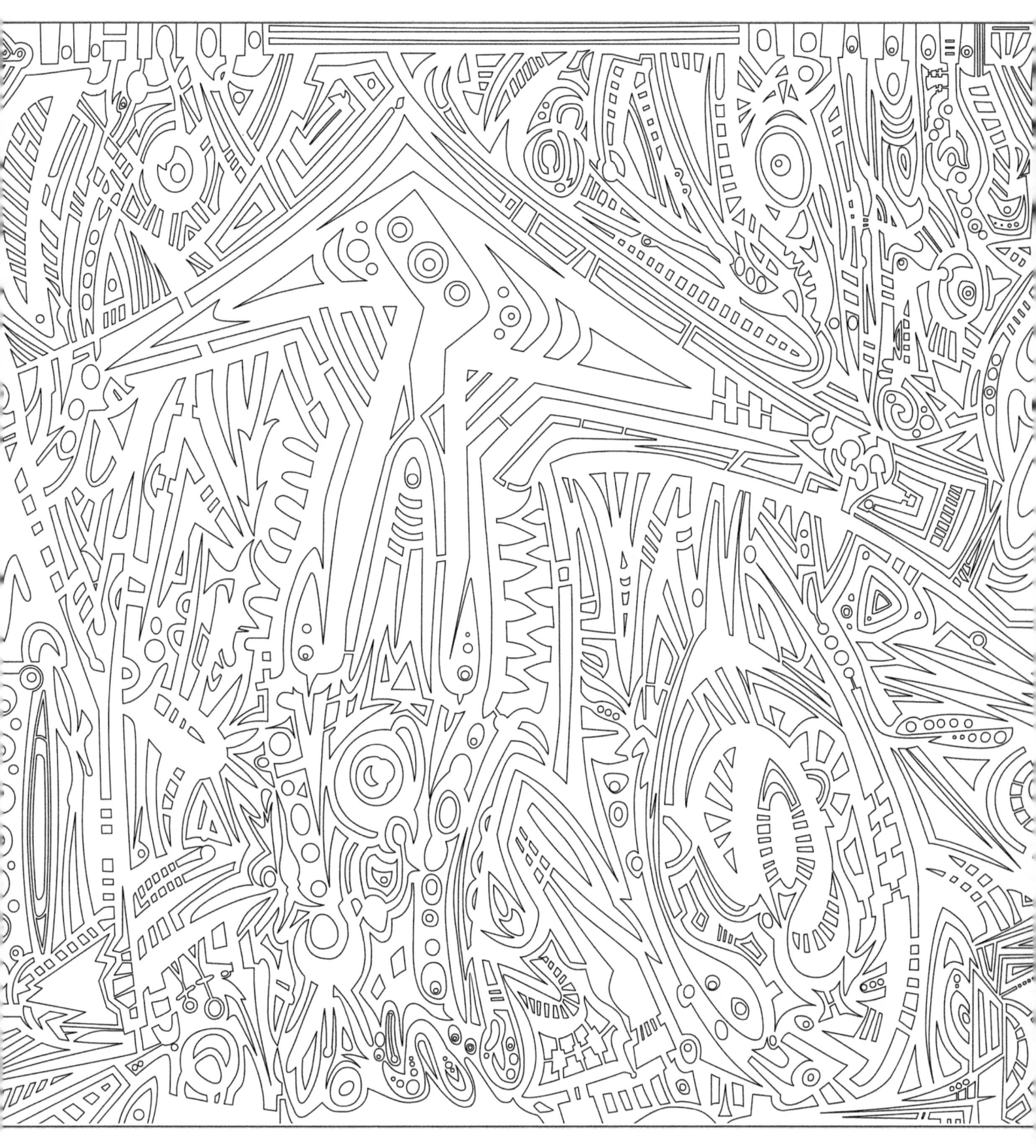

PART SIX

FORGIVABLE WHIMSY   >>

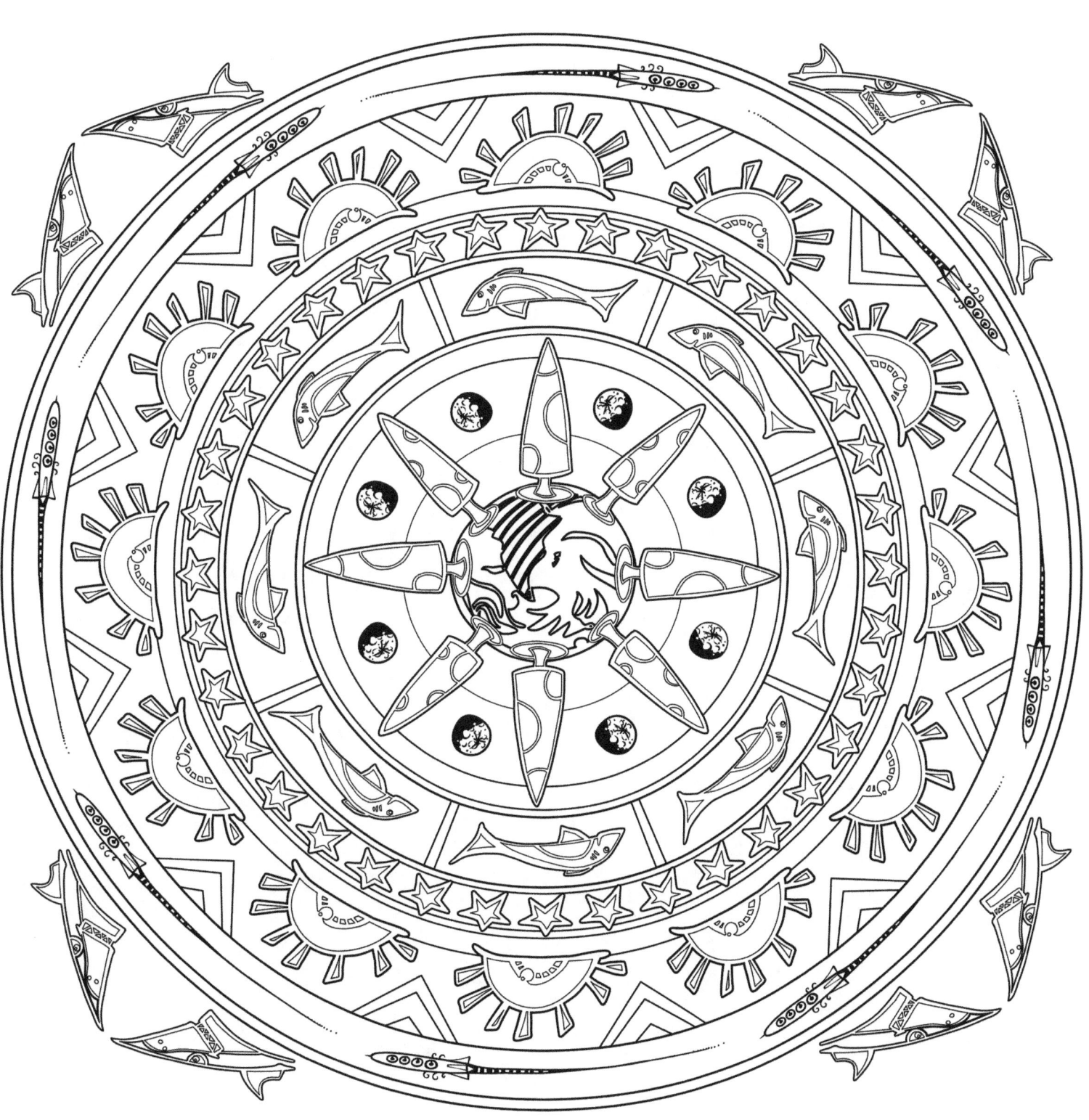

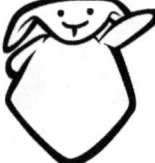

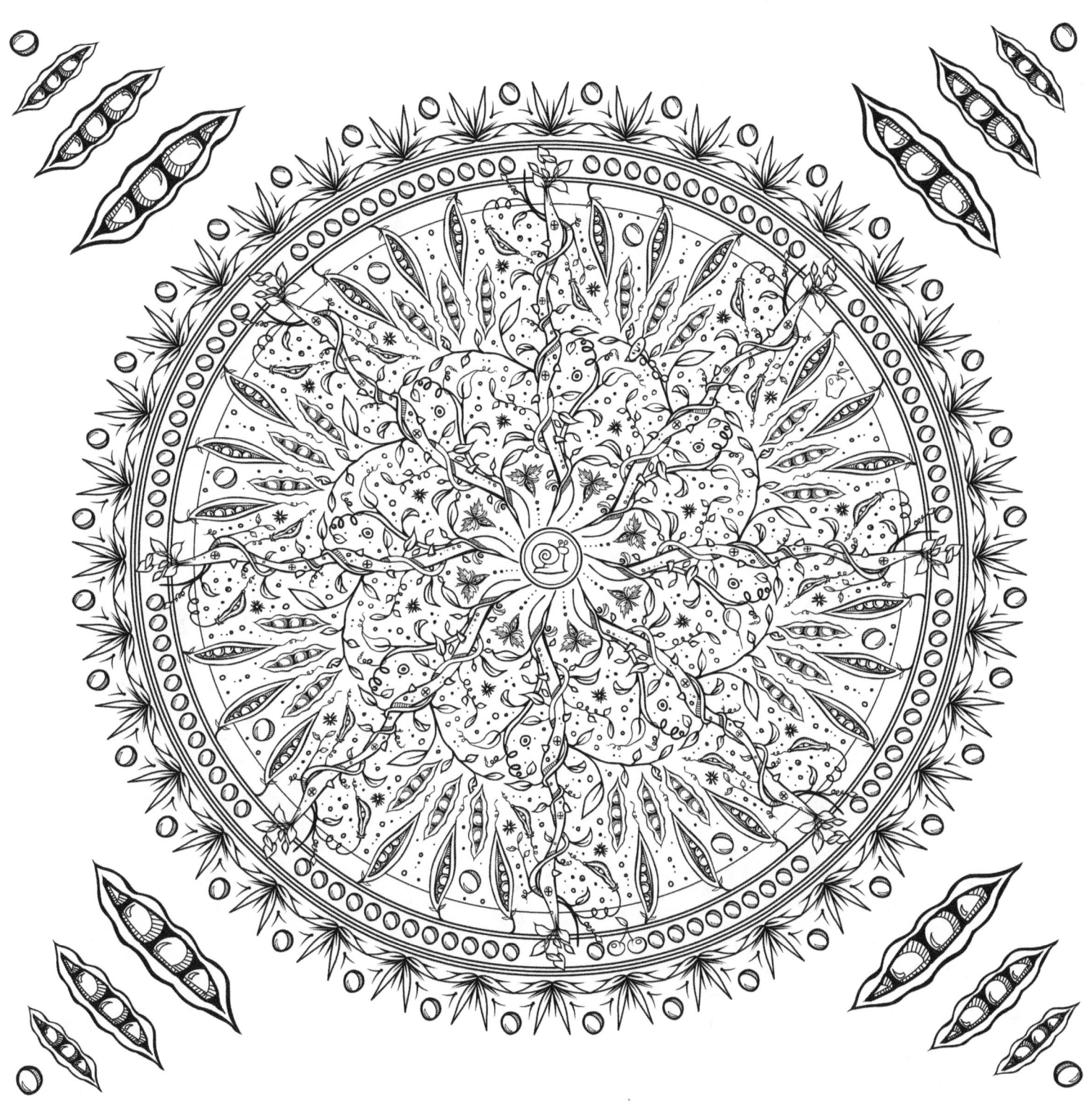

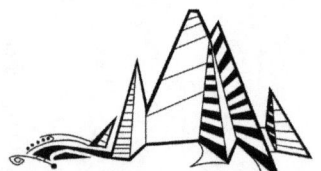

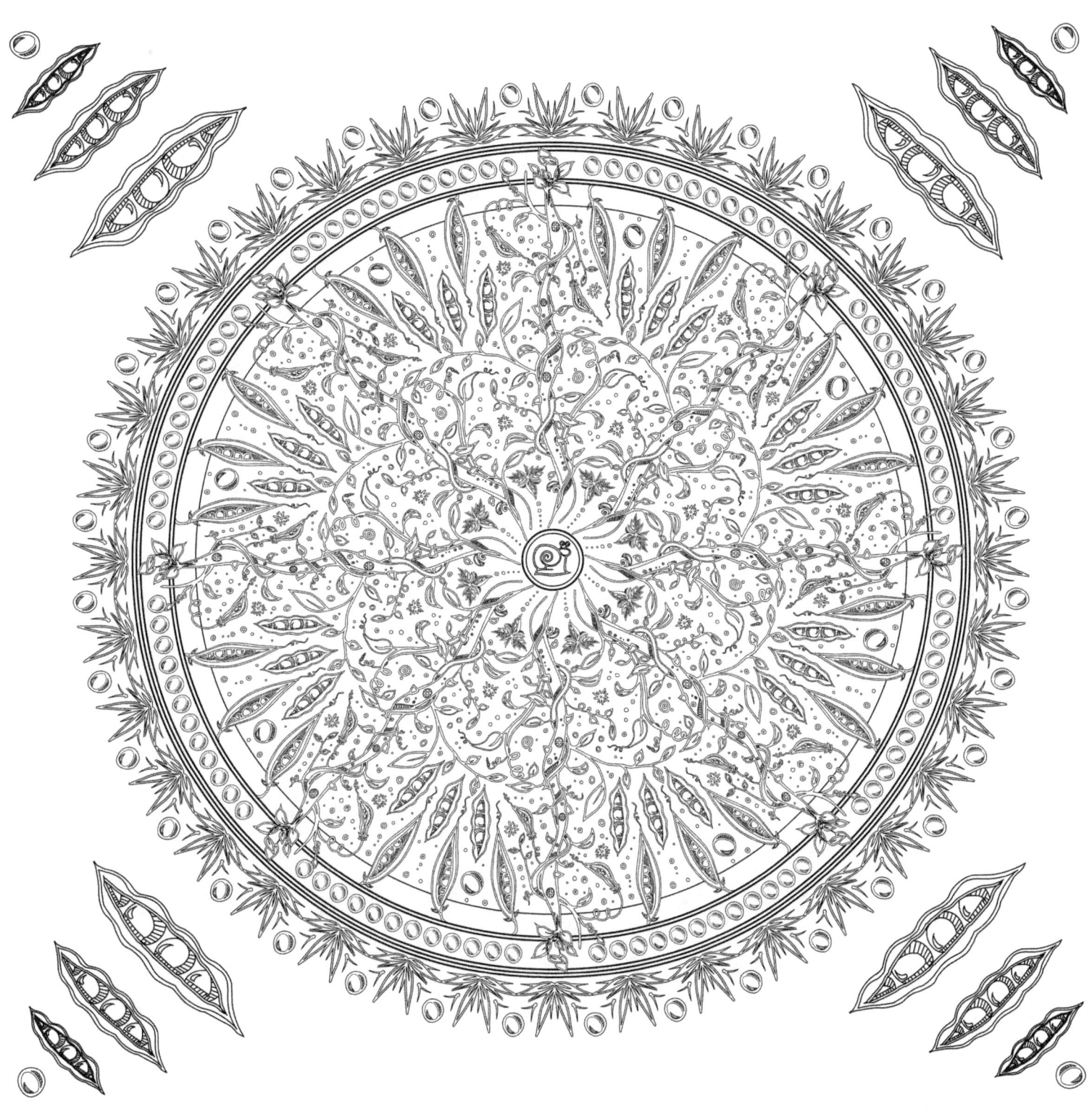

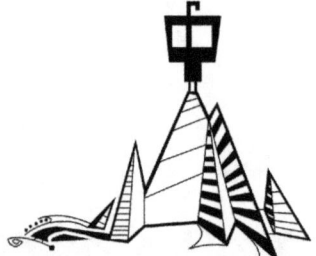

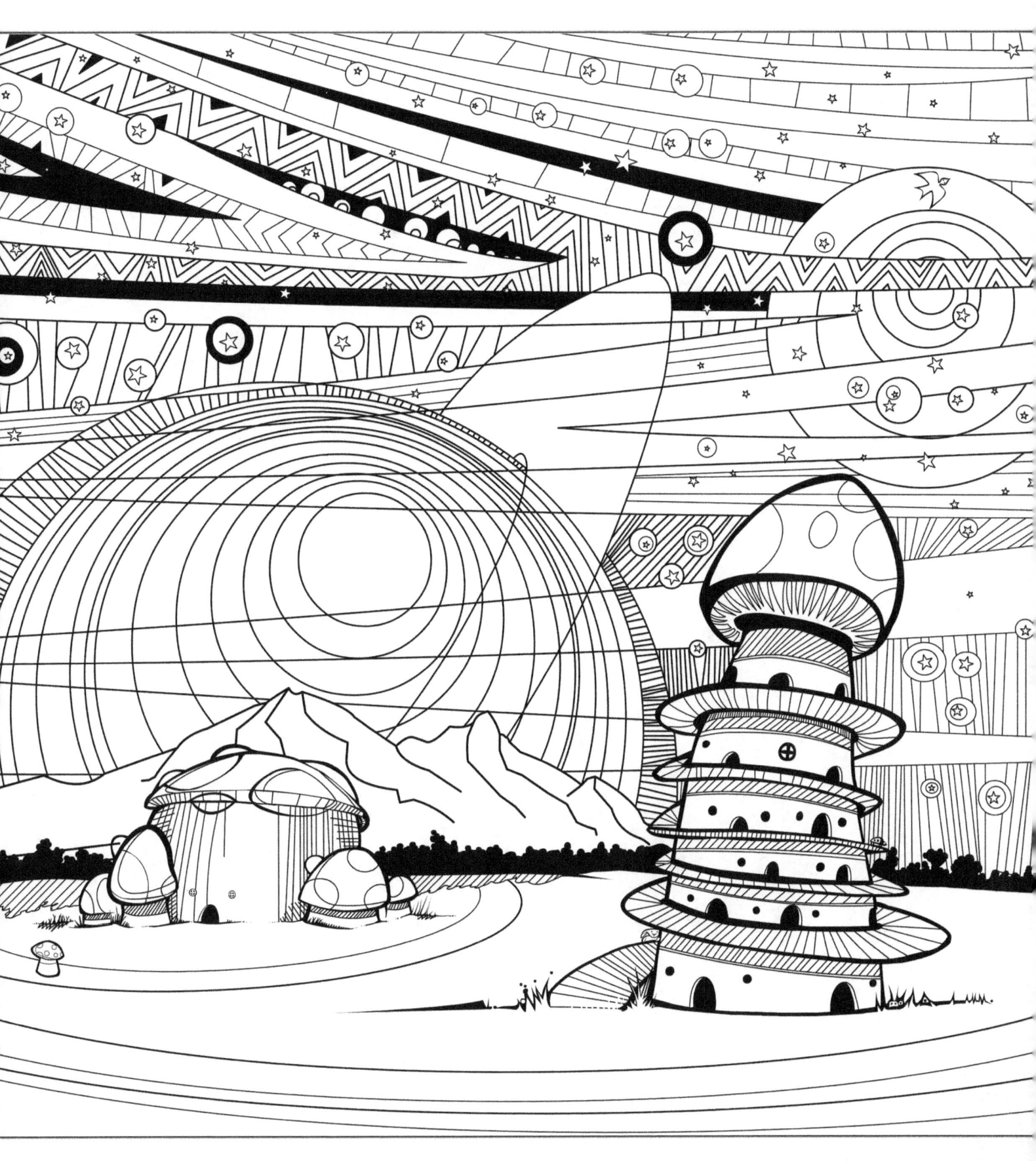

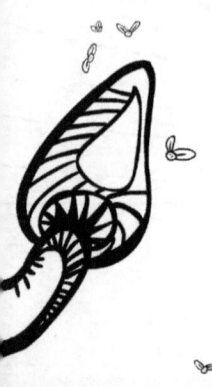

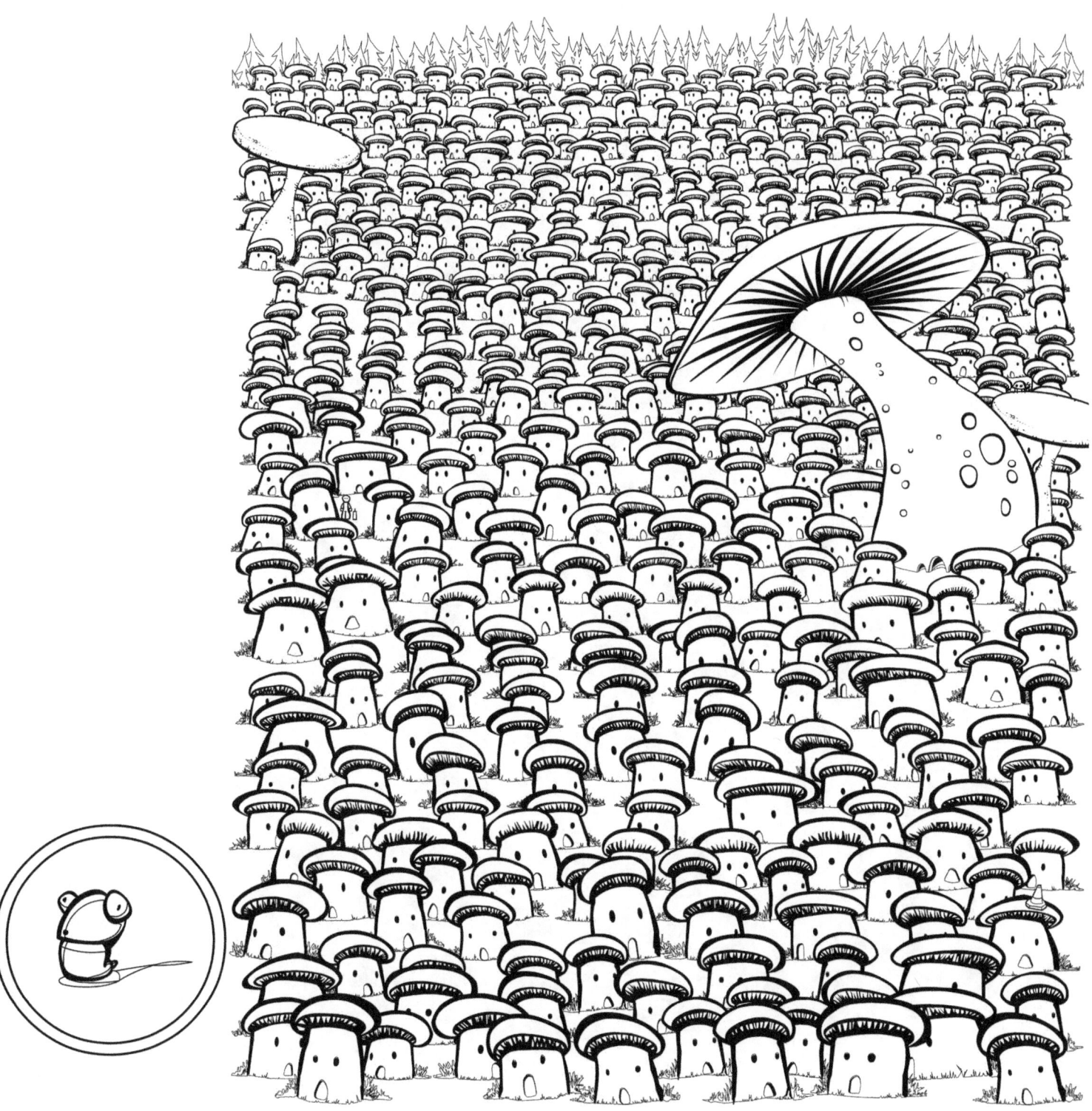

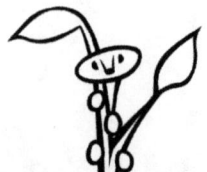

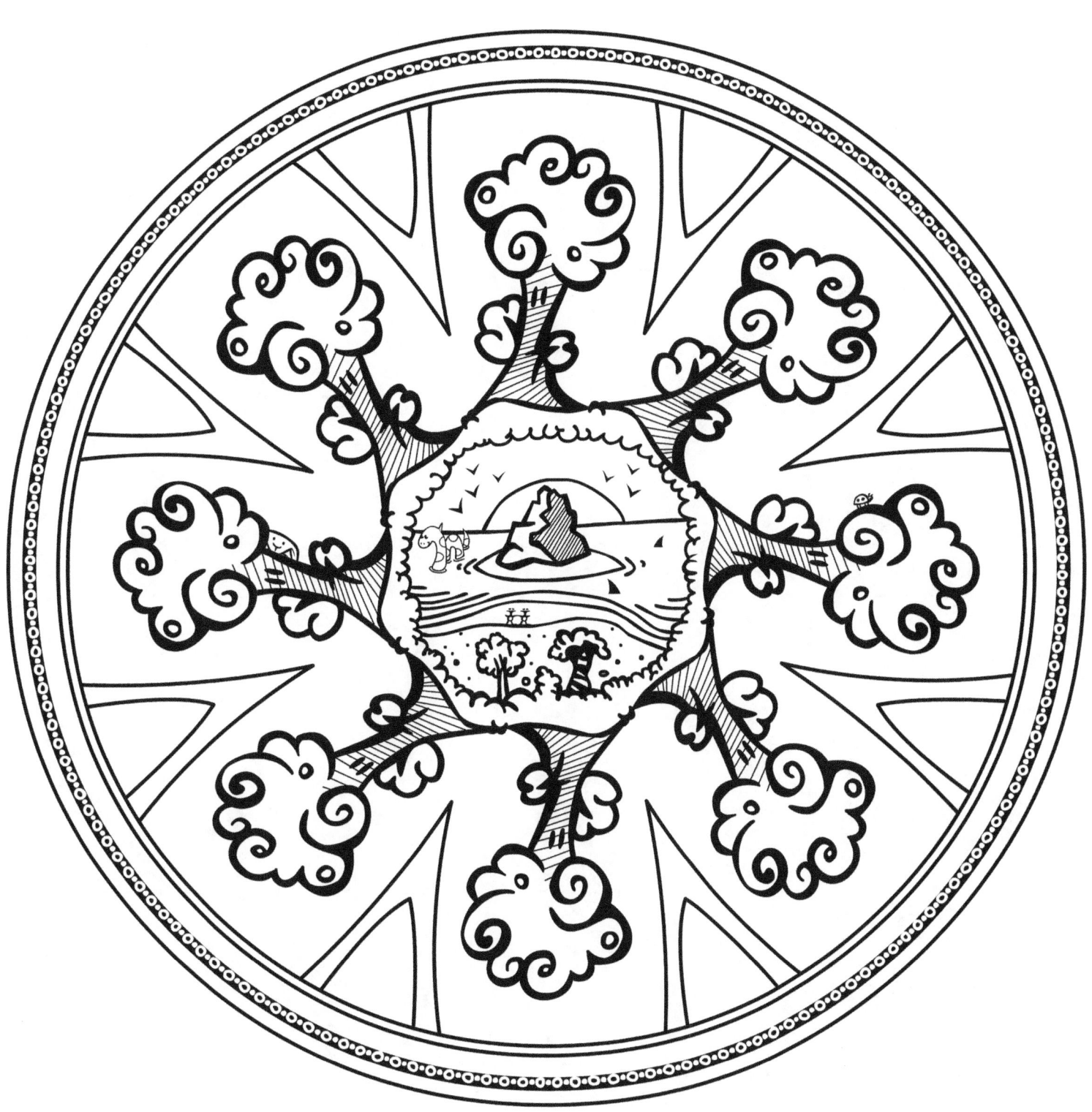

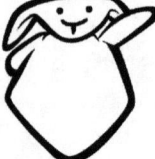

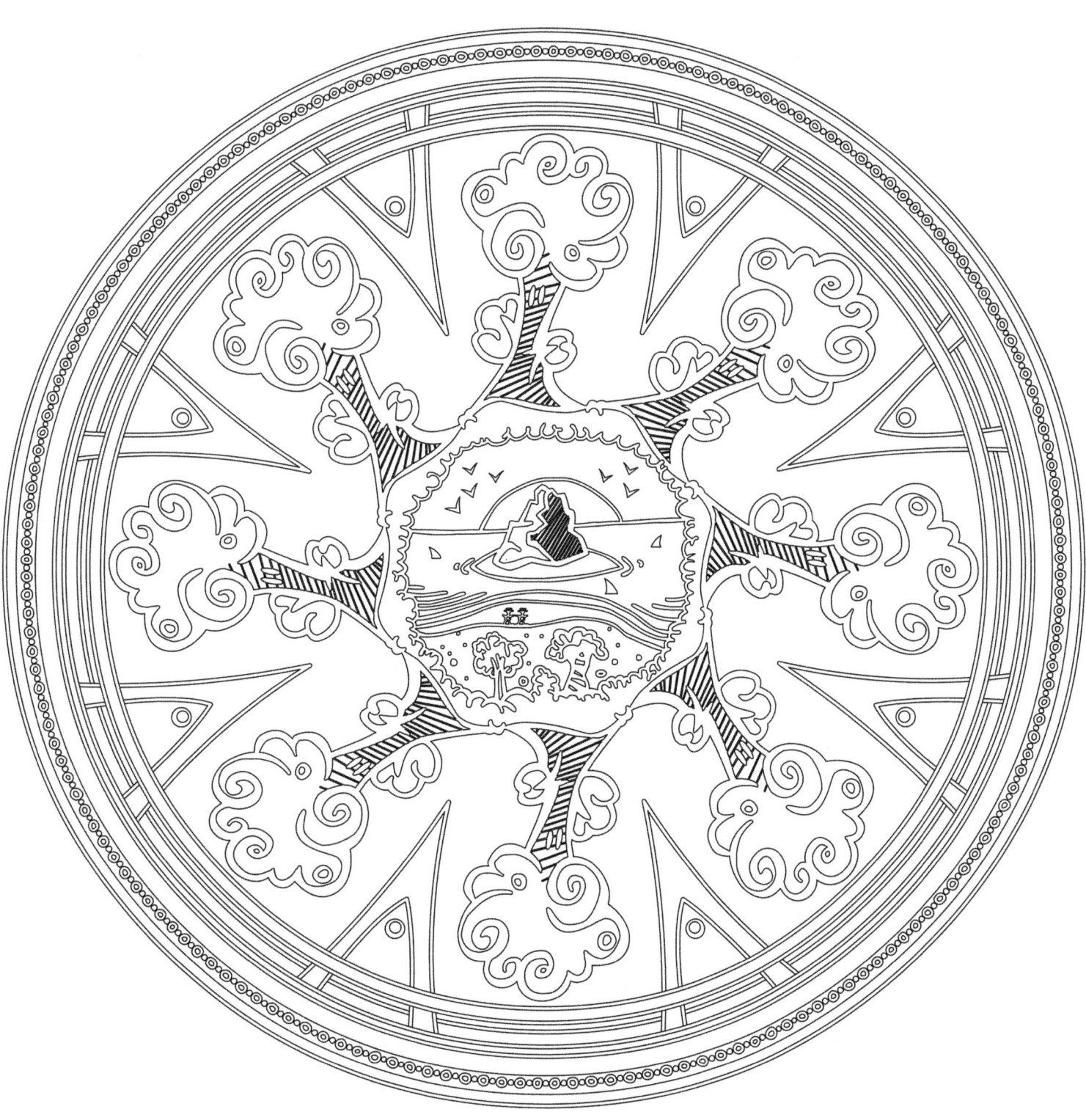

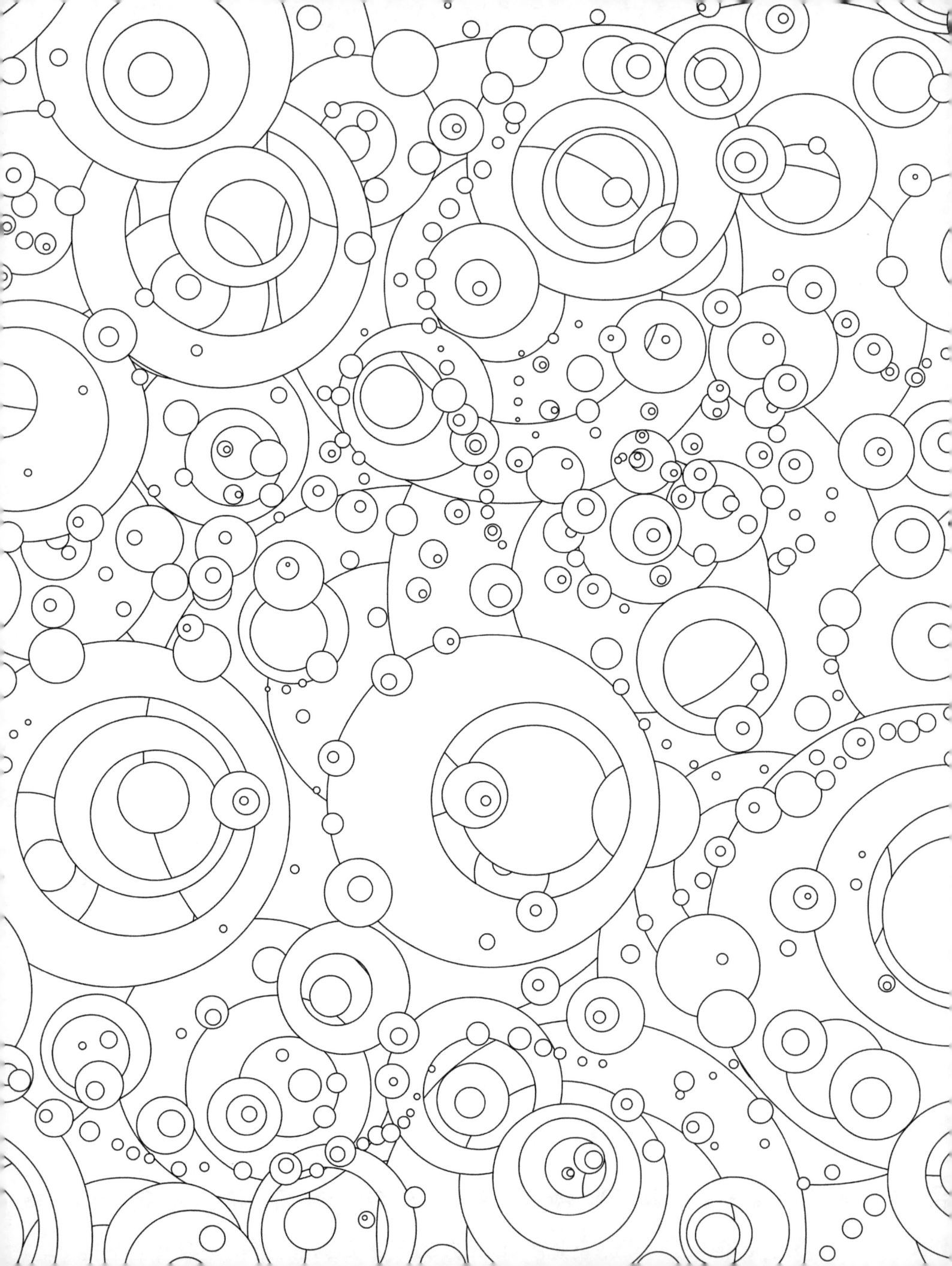

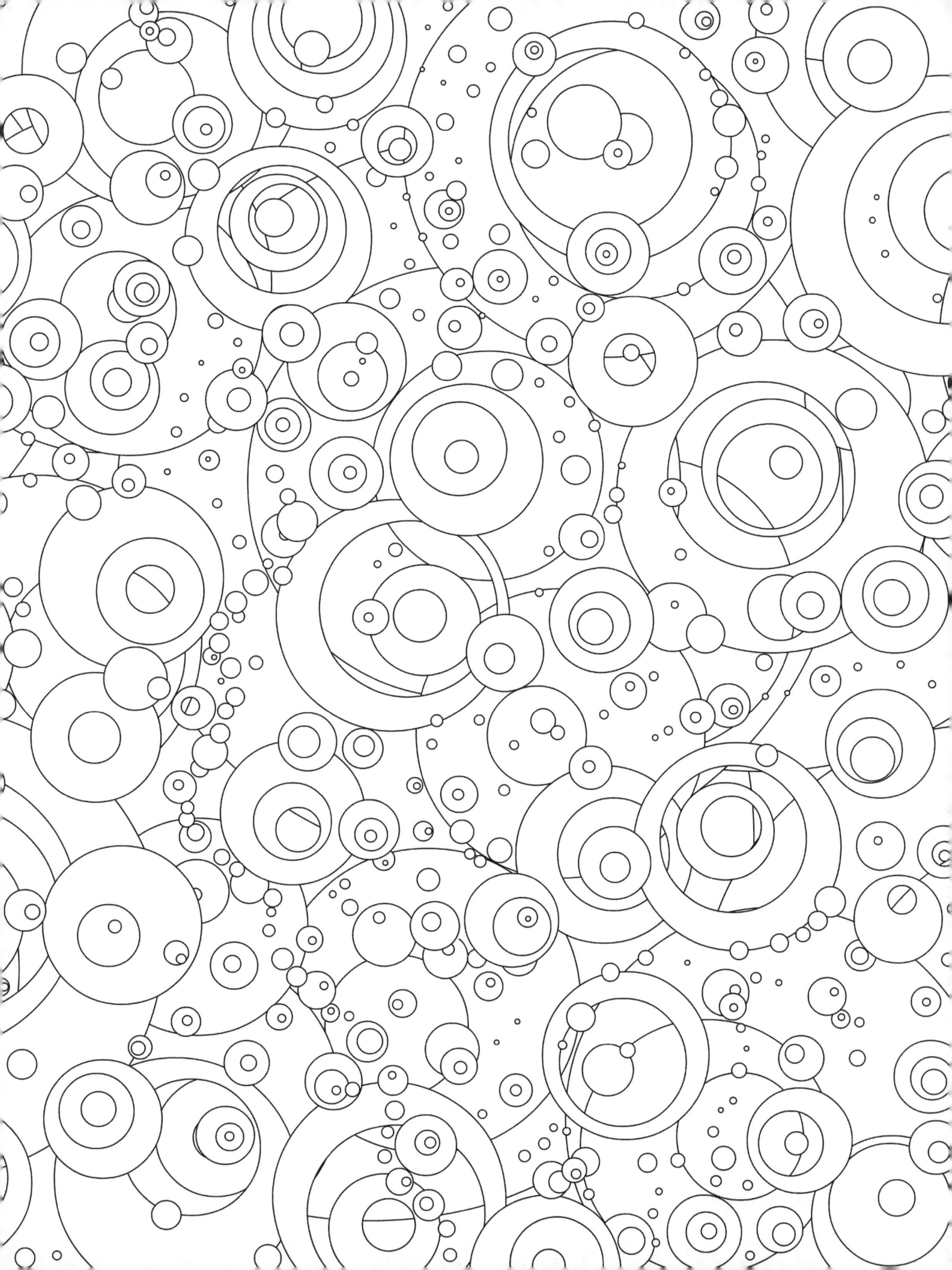

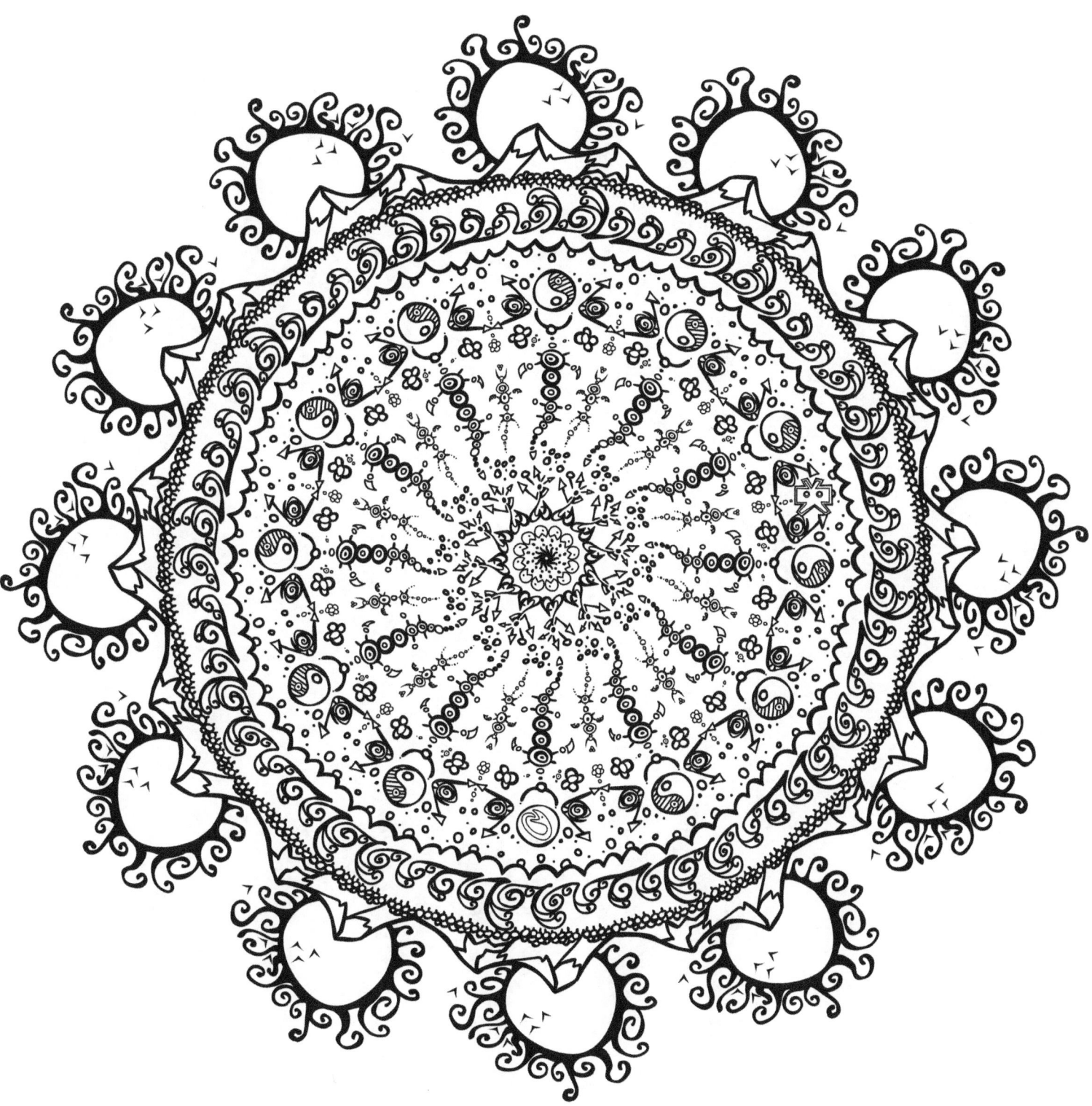

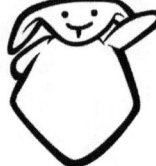

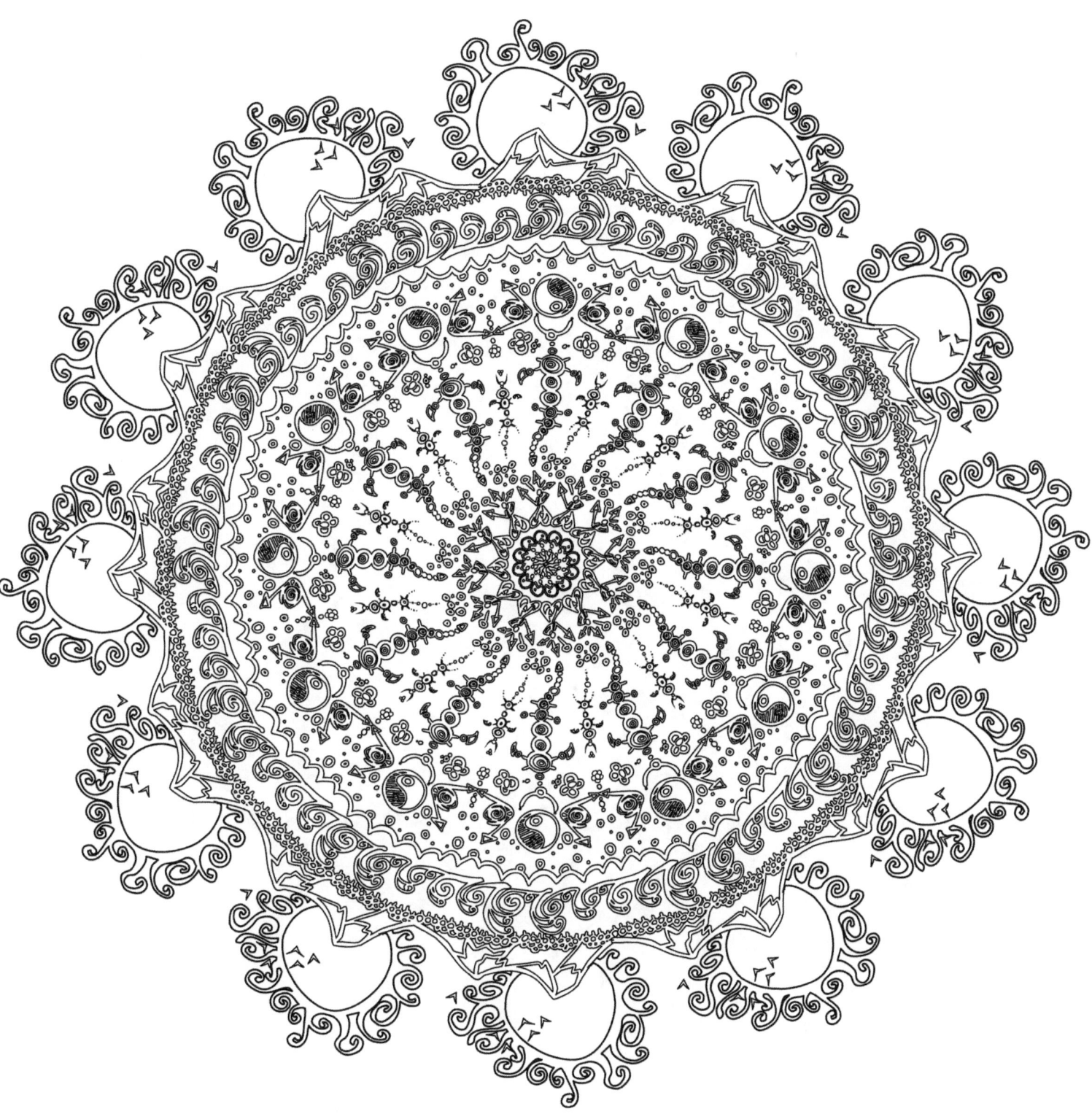

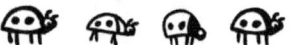

PART SEVEN

FUTURE SAMPLES...   >>
SOME BONUS BITS AND PIECES FROM UPCOMING PROJECTS

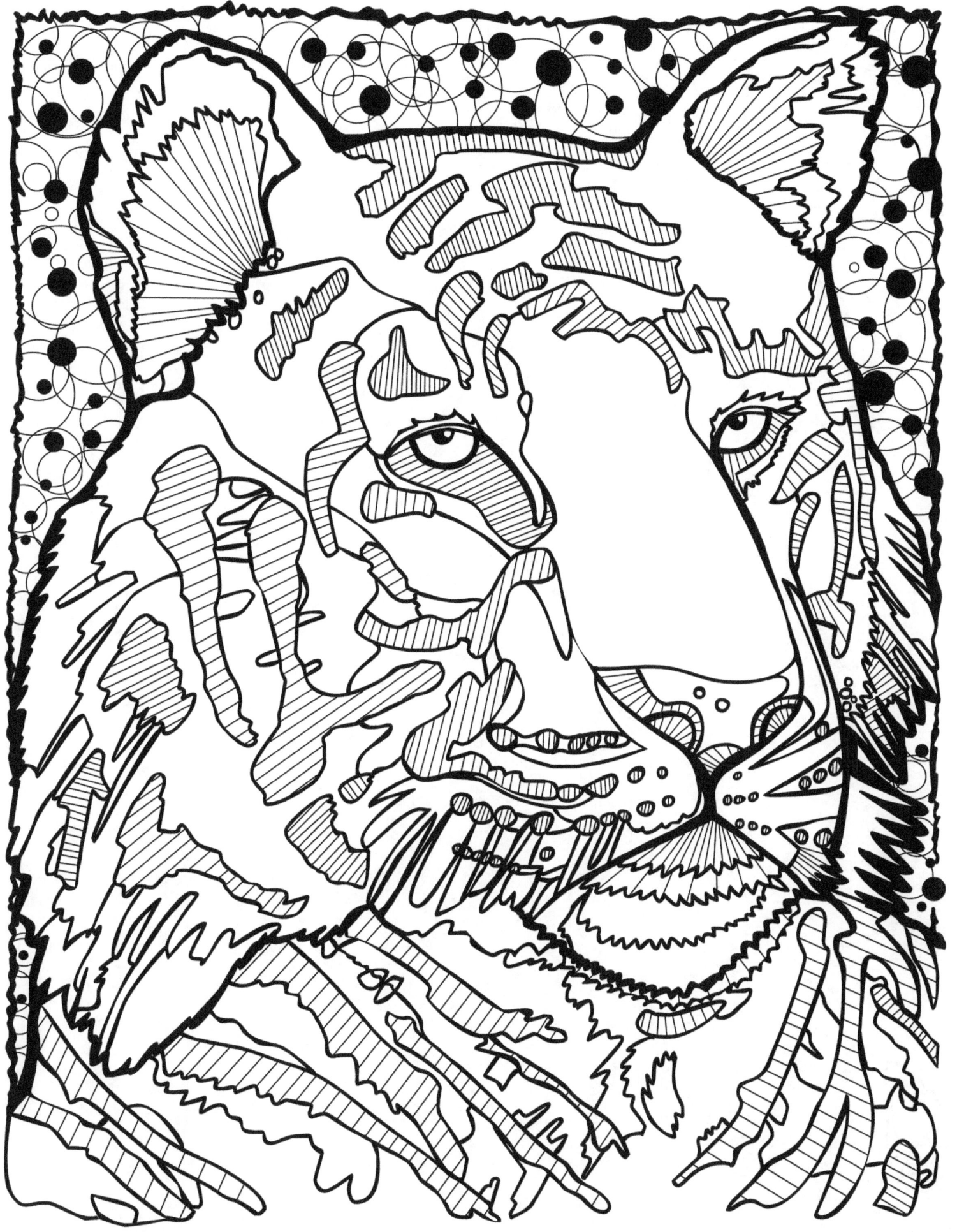

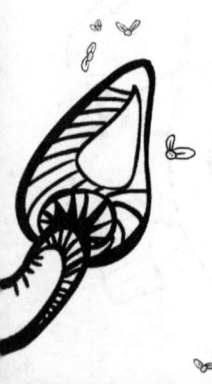

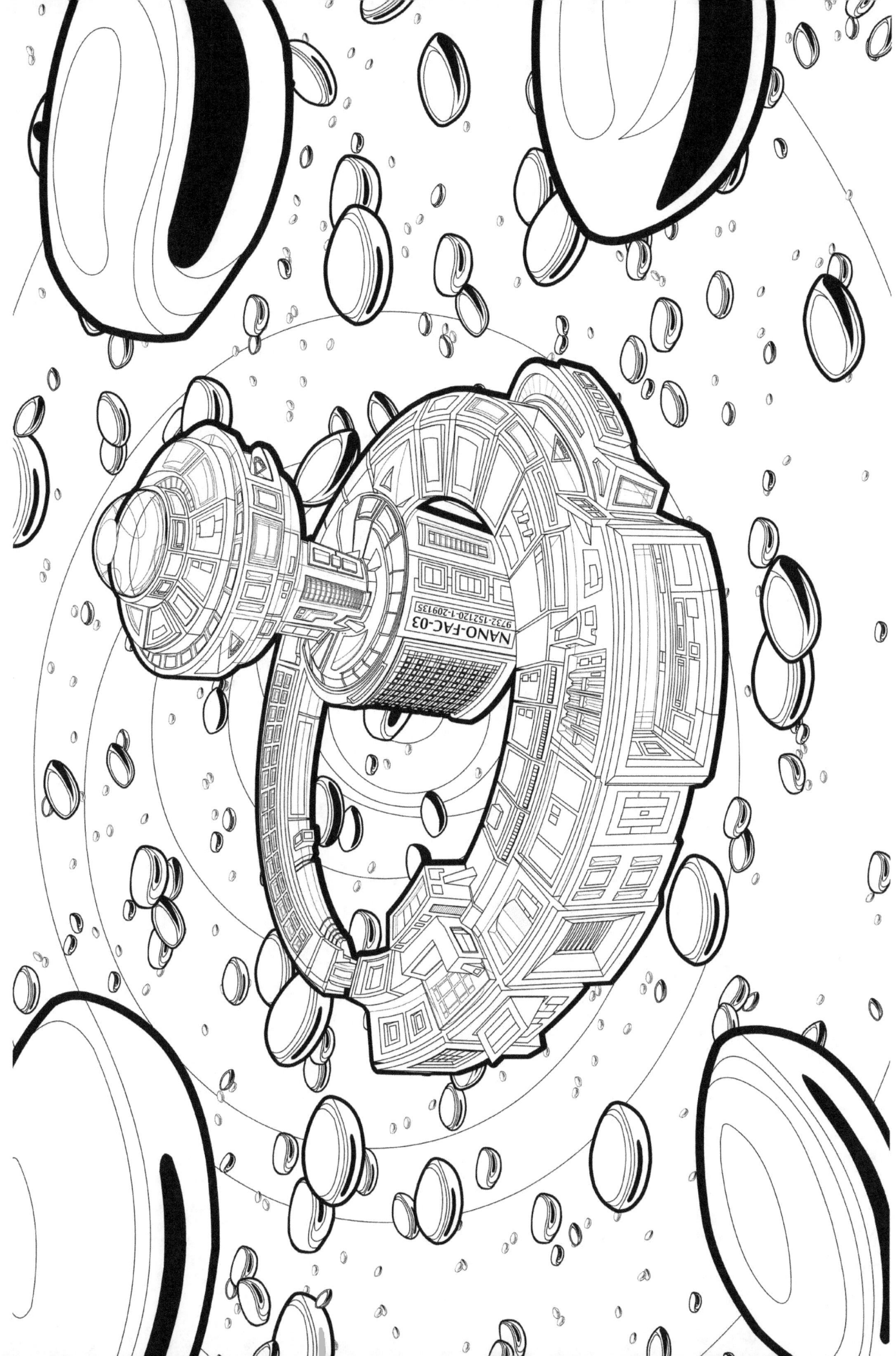

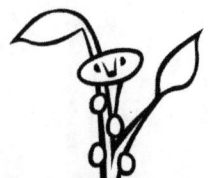

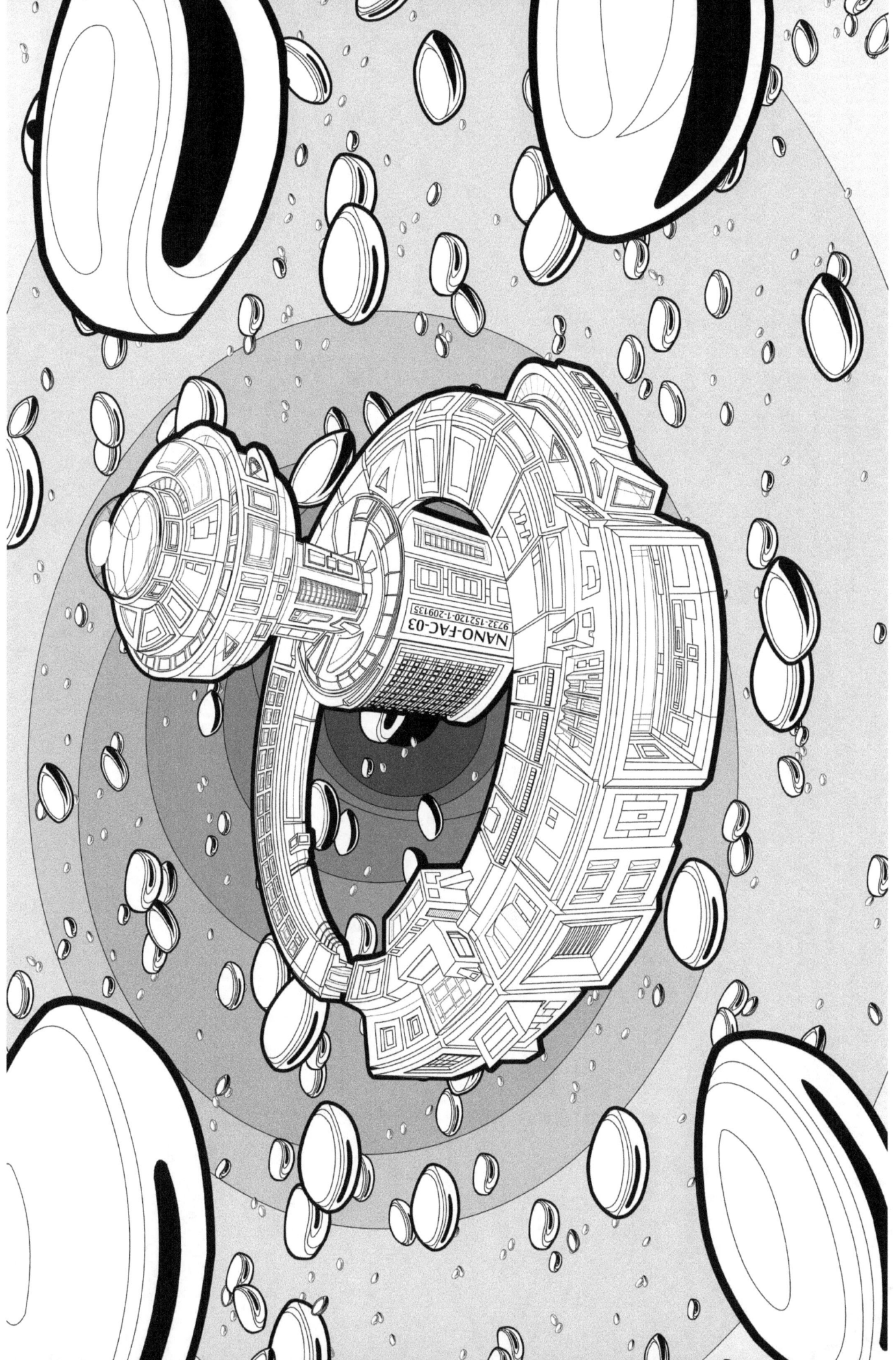

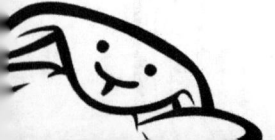

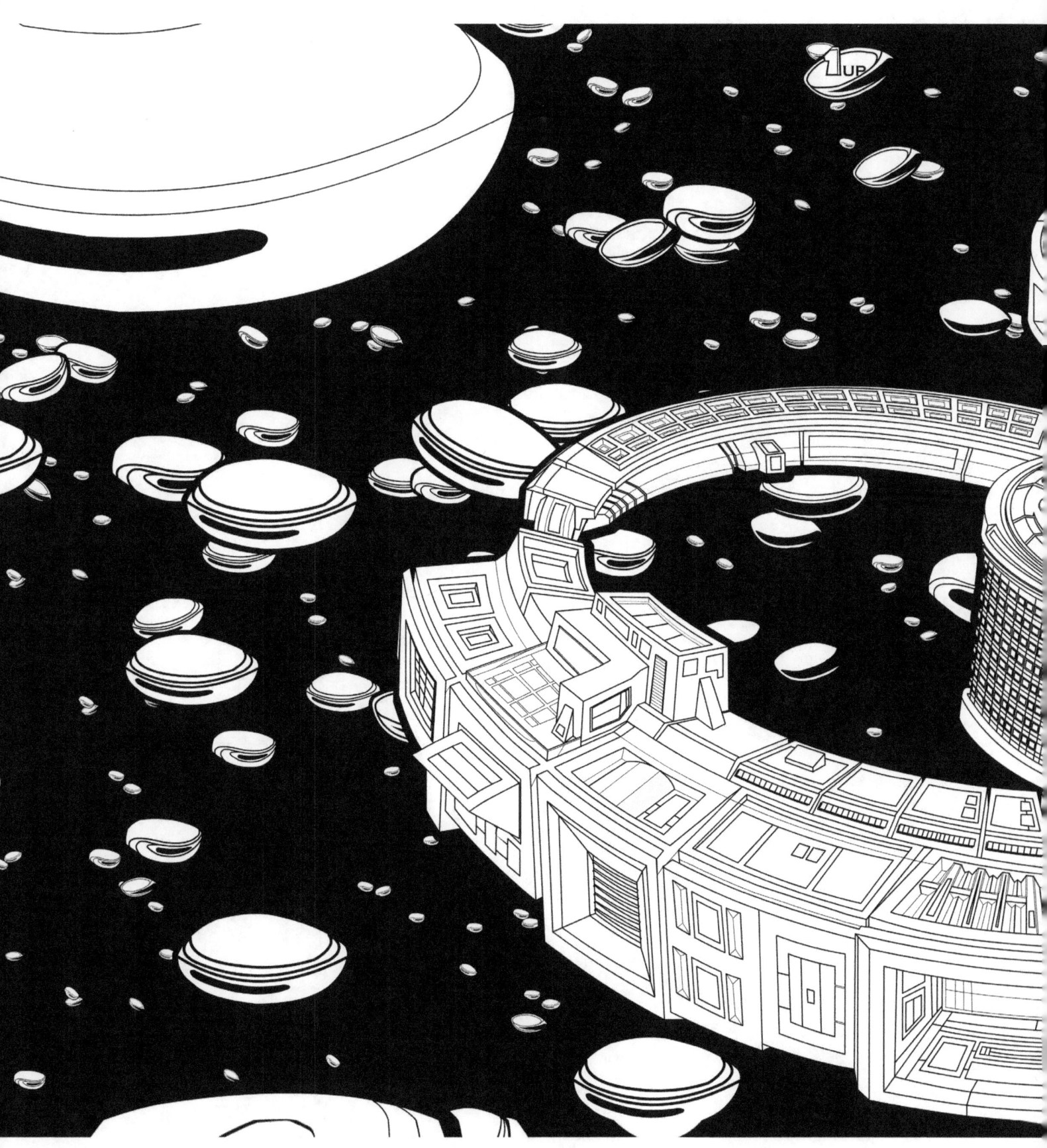

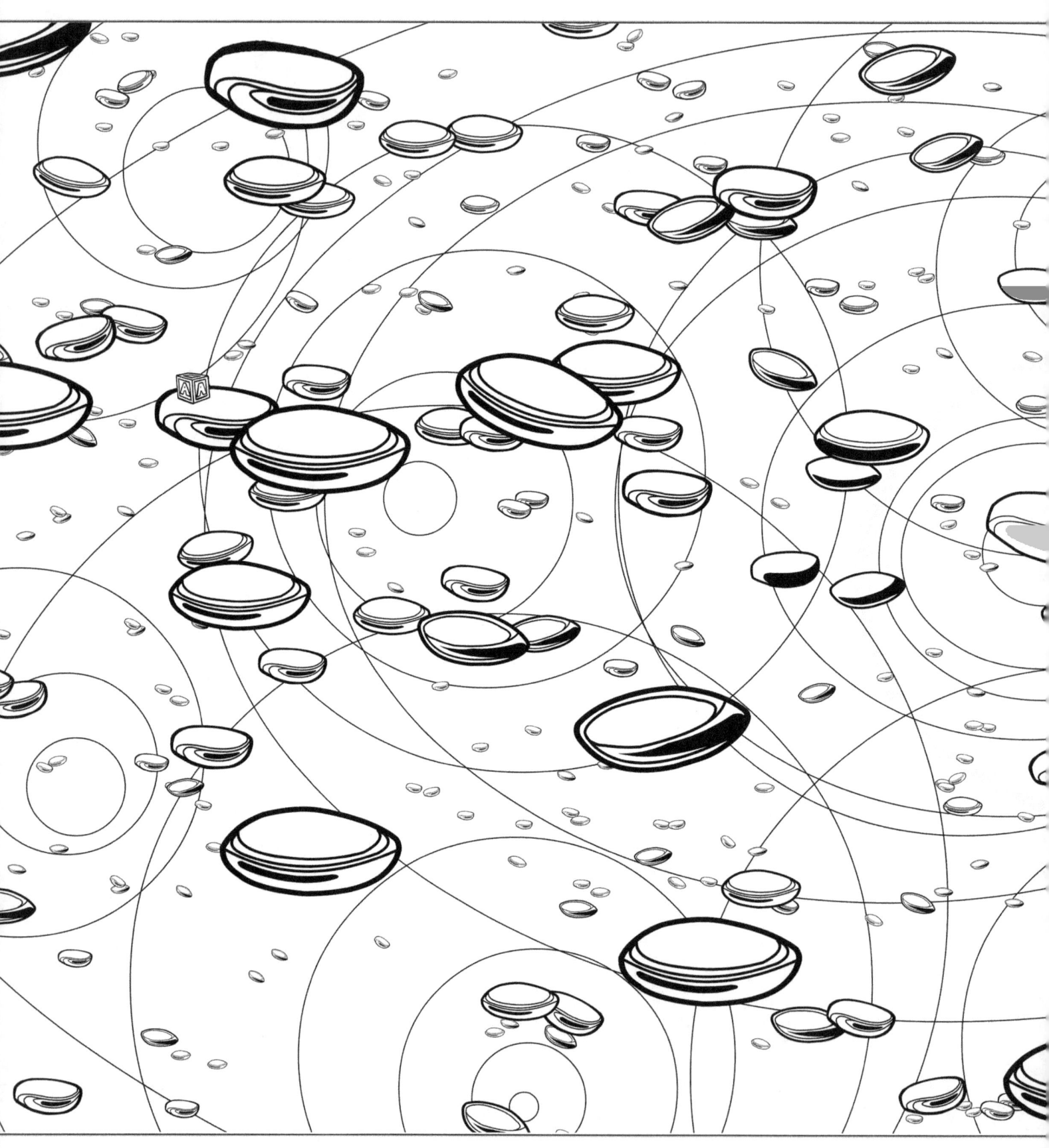

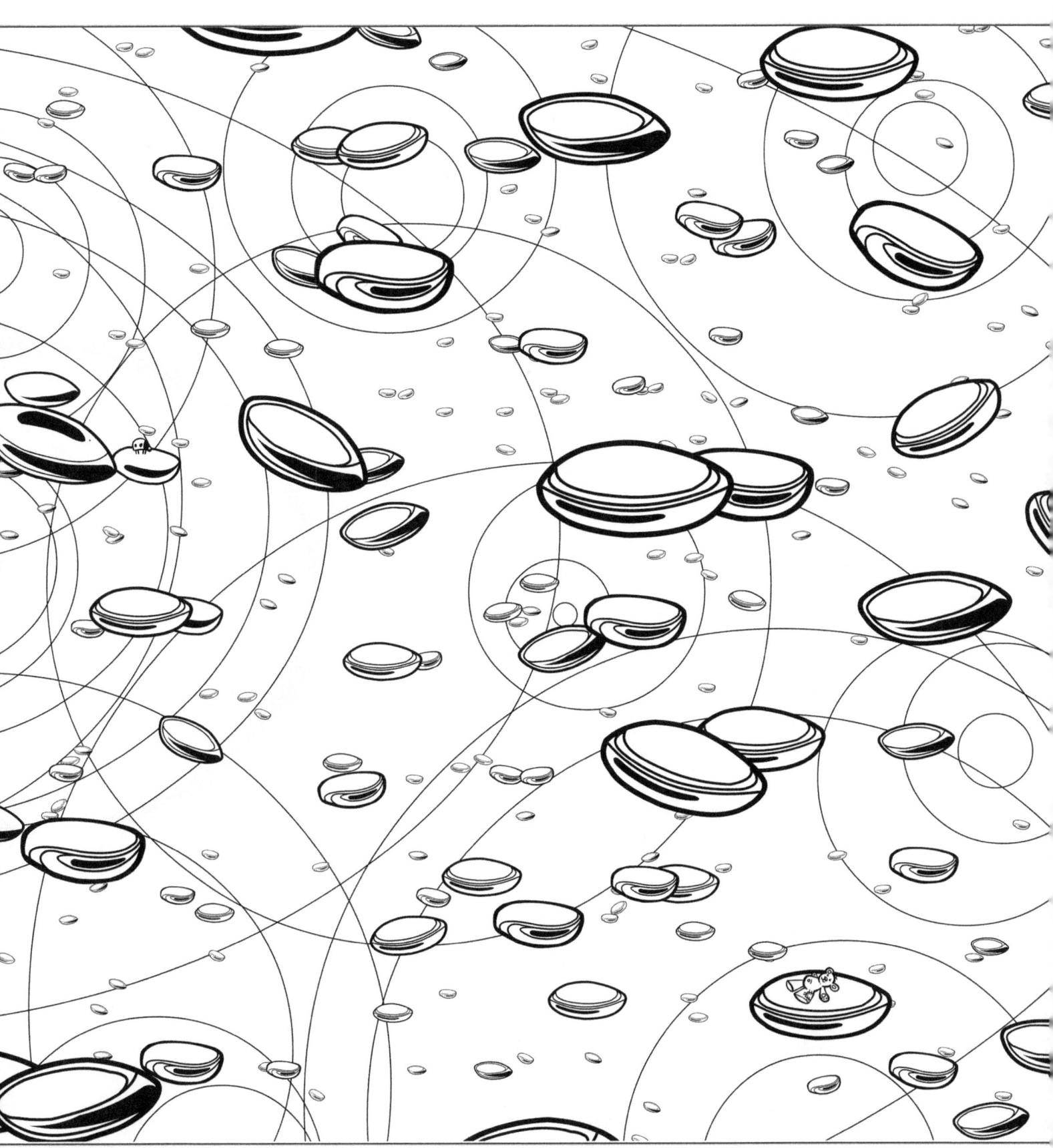

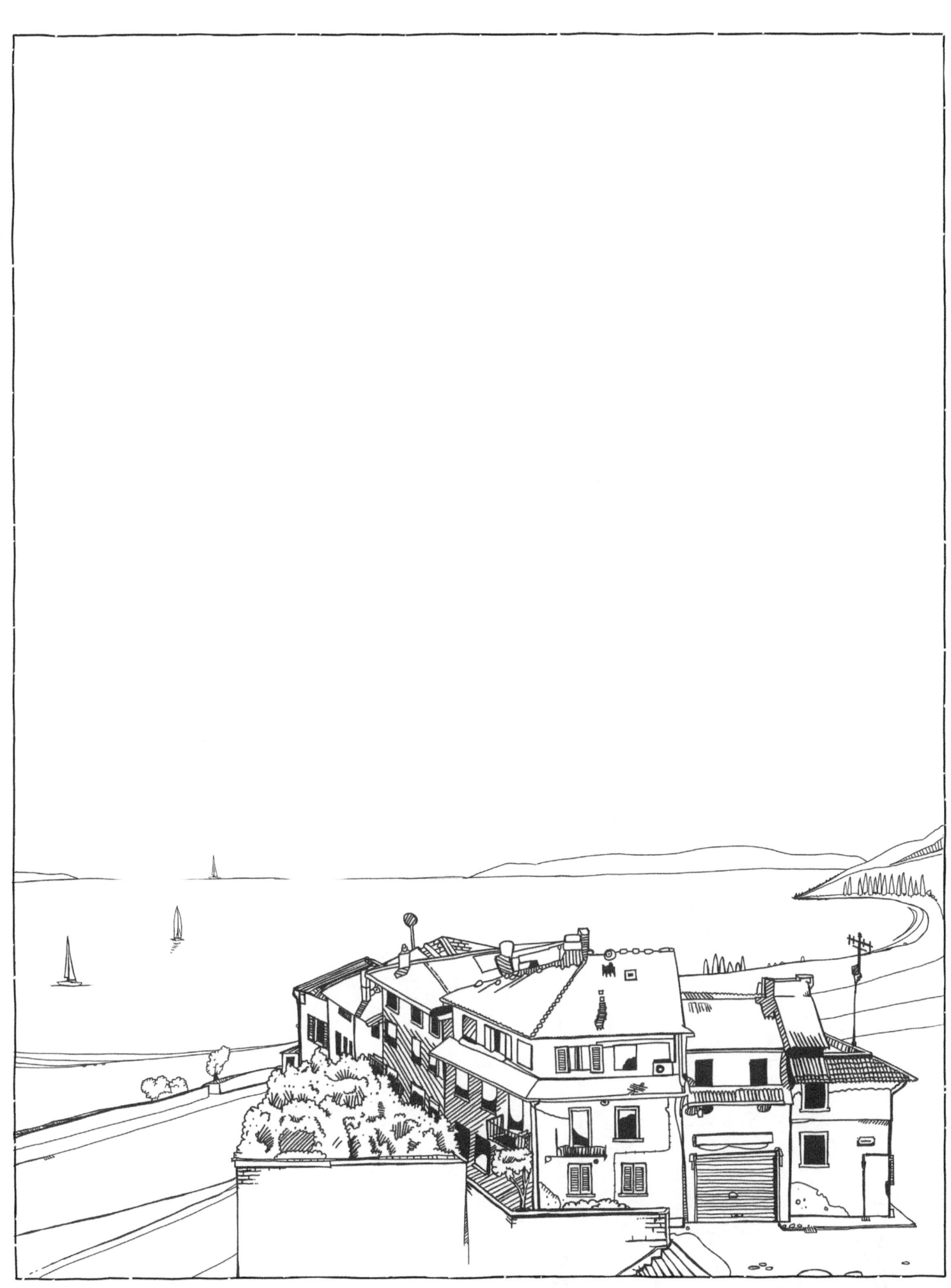

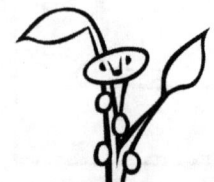

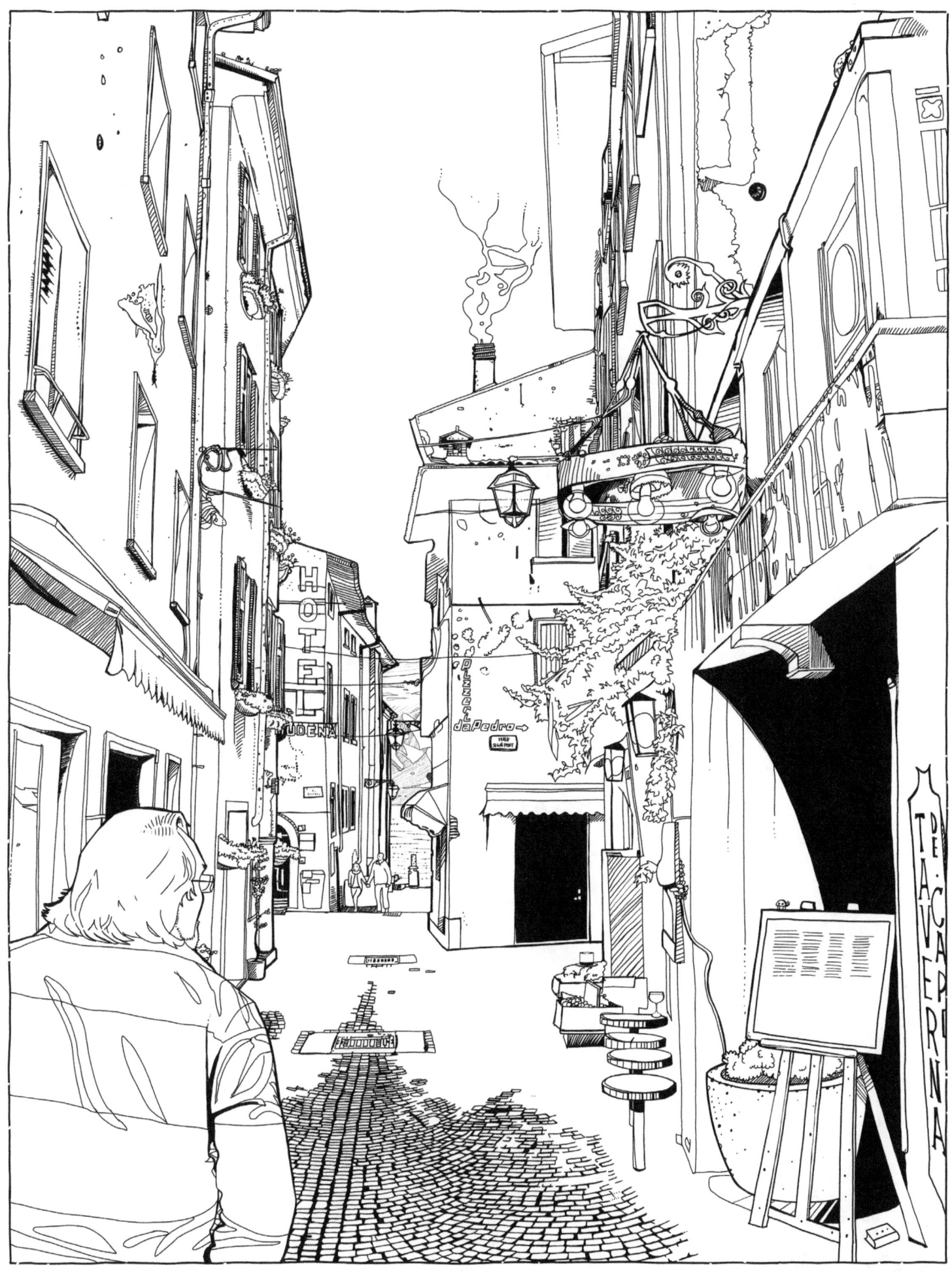

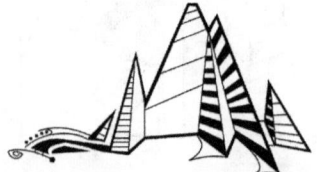

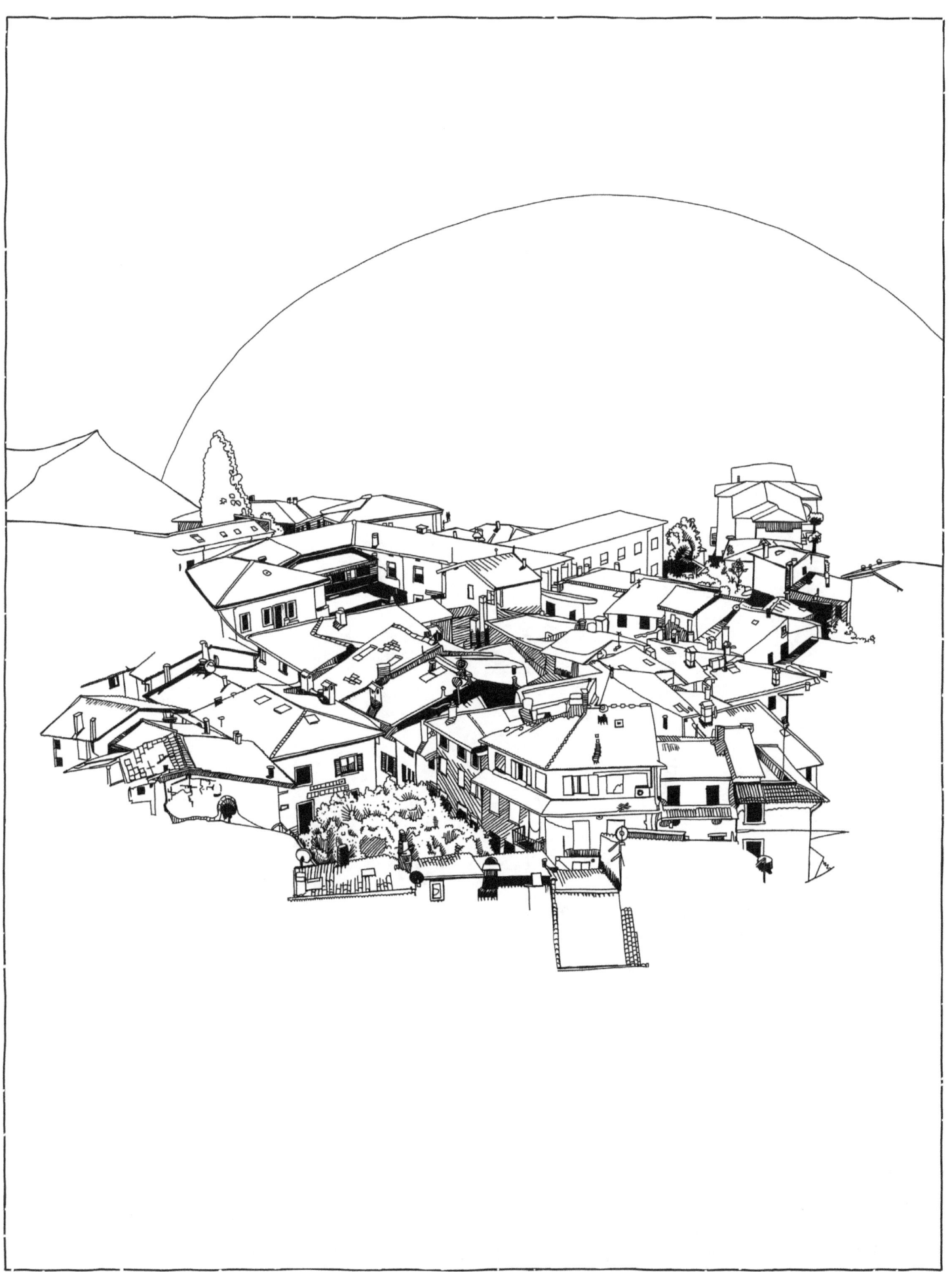

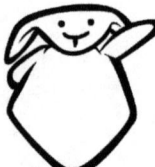

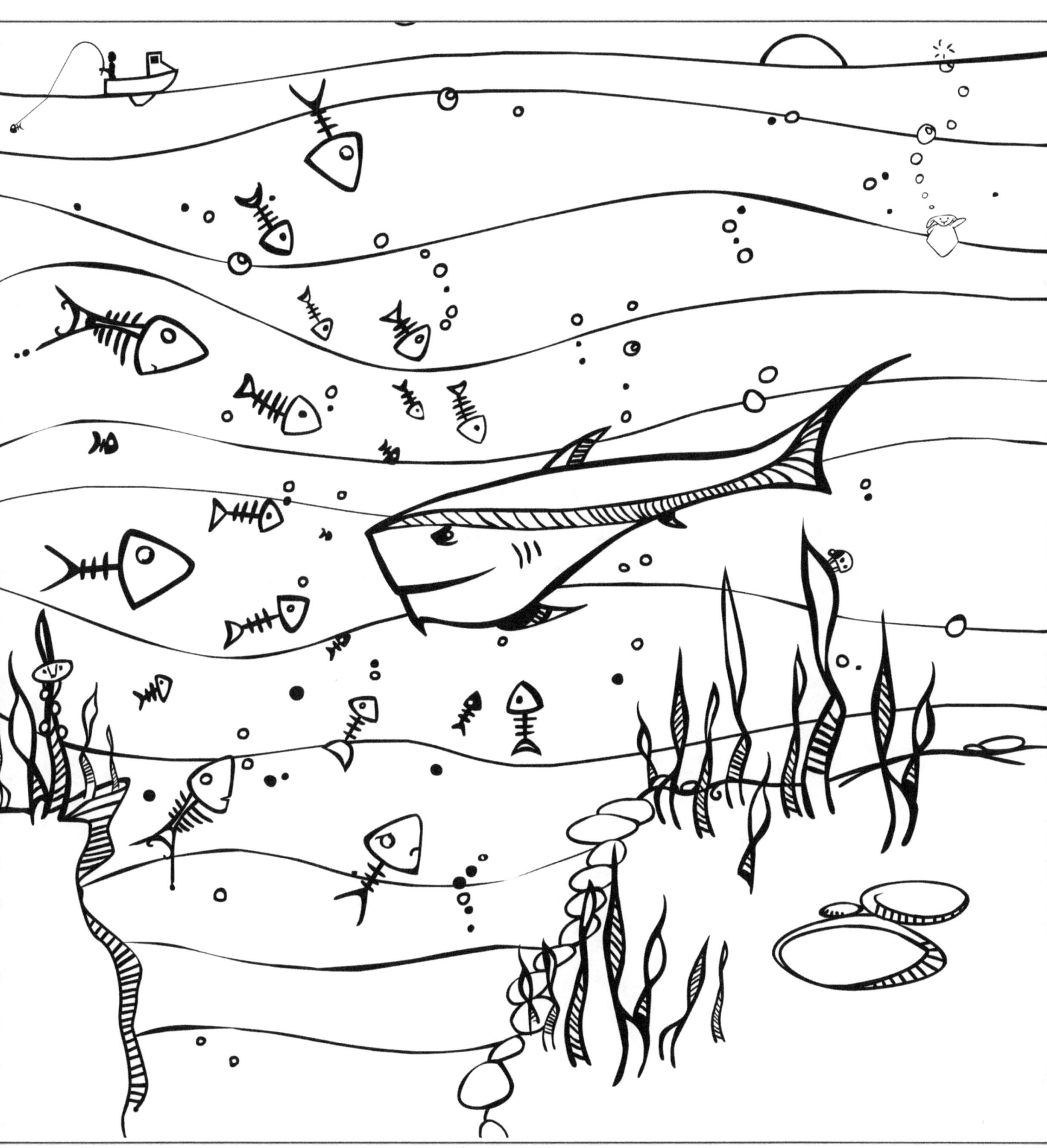

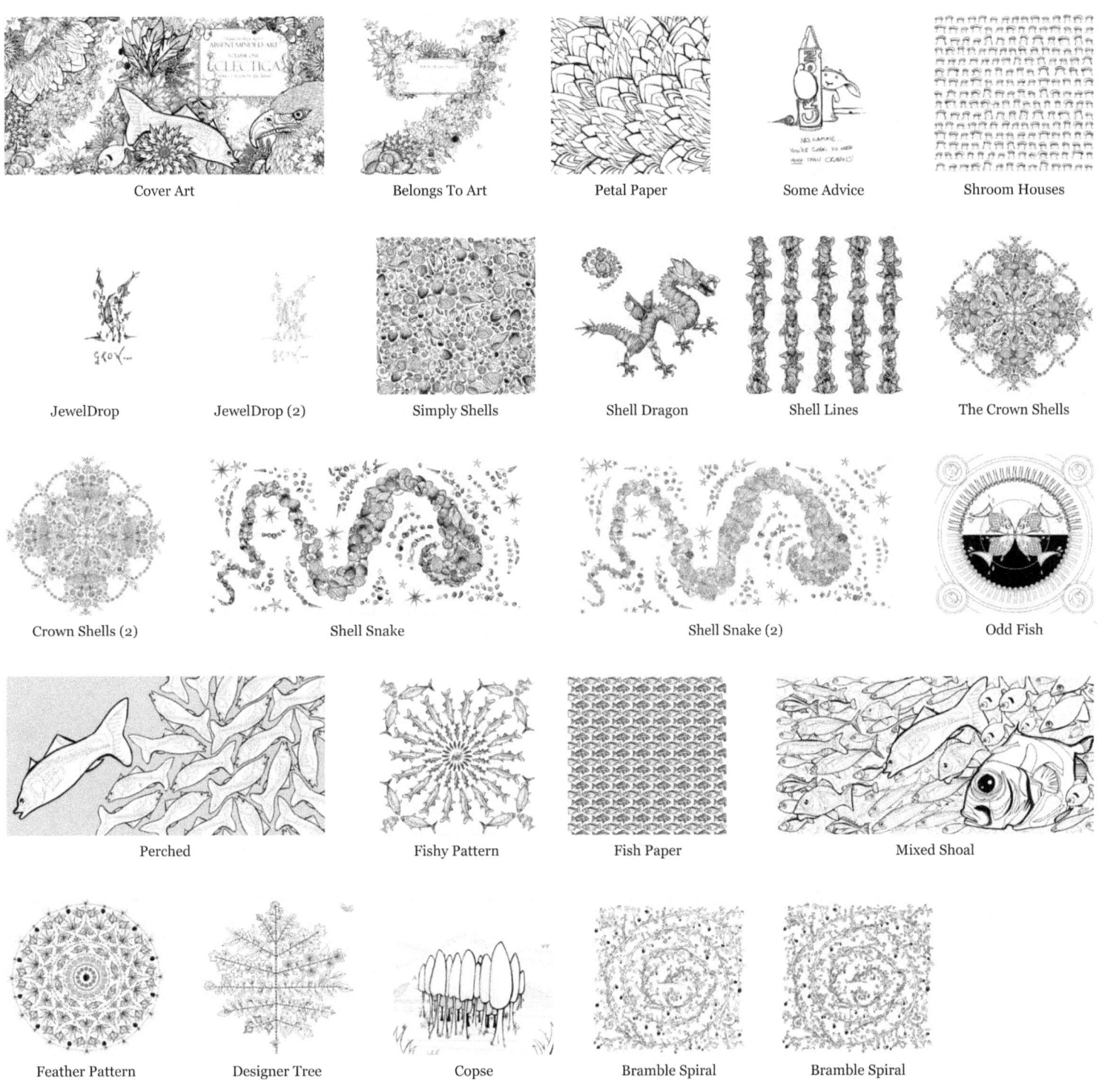

Cover Art

Belongs To Art

Petal Paper

Some Advice

Shroom Houses

JewelDrop

JewelDrop (2)

Simply Shells

Shell Dragon

Shell Lines

The Crown Shells

Crown Shells (2)

Shell Snake

Shell Snake (2)

Odd Fish

Perched

Fishy Pattern

Fish Paper

Mixed Shoal

Feather Pattern

Designer Tree

Copse

Bramble Spiral

Bramble Spiral

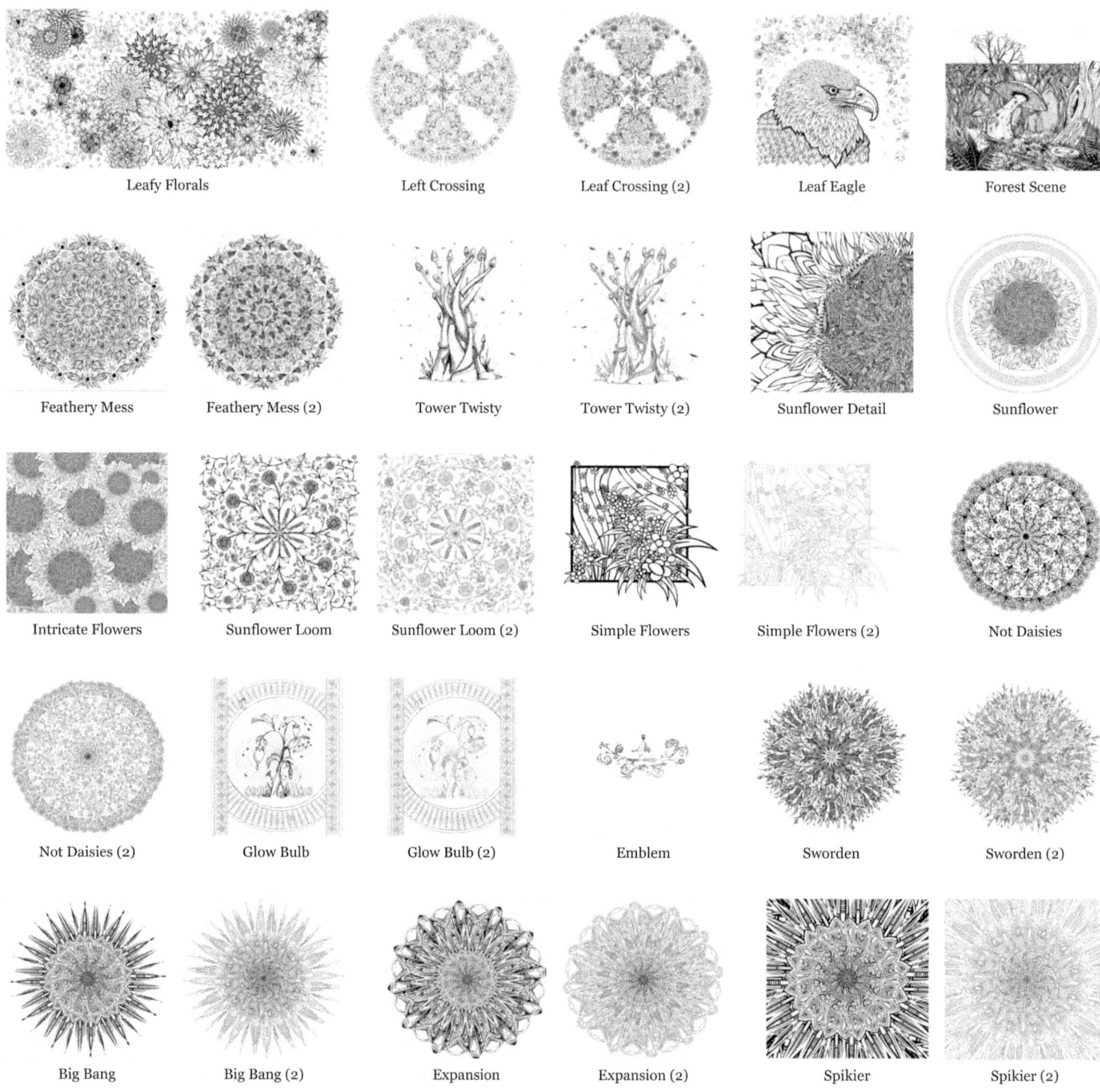

Leafy Florals

Left Crossing

Leaf Crossing (2)

Leaf Eagle

Forest Scene

Feathery Mess

Feathery Mess (2)

Tower Twisty

Tower Twisty (2)

Sunflower Detail

Sunflower

Intricate Flowers

Sunflower Loom

Sunflower Loom (2)

Simple Flowers

Simple Flowers (2)

Not Daisies

Not Daisies (2)

Glow Bulb

Glow Bulb (2)

Emblem

Sworden

Sworden (2)

Big Bang

Big Bang (2)

Expansion

Expansion (2)

Spikier

Spikier (2)

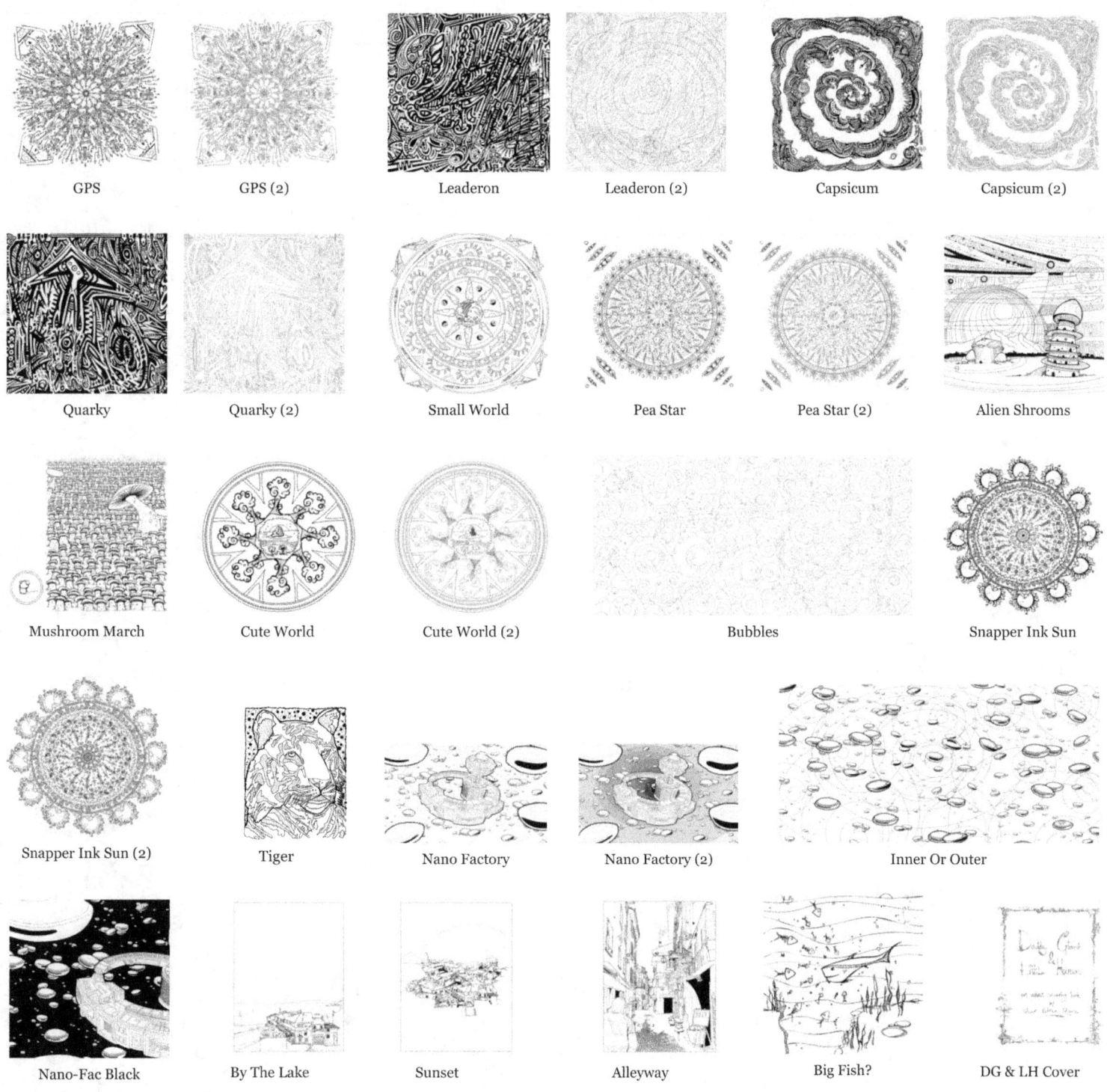

GPS

GPS (2)

Leaderon

Leaderon (2)

Capsicum

Capsicum (2)

Quarky

Quarky (2)

Small World

Pea Star

Pea Star (2)

Alien Shrooms

Mushroom March

Cute World

Cute World (2)

Bubbles

Snapper Ink Sun

Snapper Ink Sun (2)

Tiger

Nano Factory

Nano Factory (2)

Inner Or Outer

Nano-Fac Black

By The Lake

Sunset

Alleyway

Big Fish?

DG & LH Cover

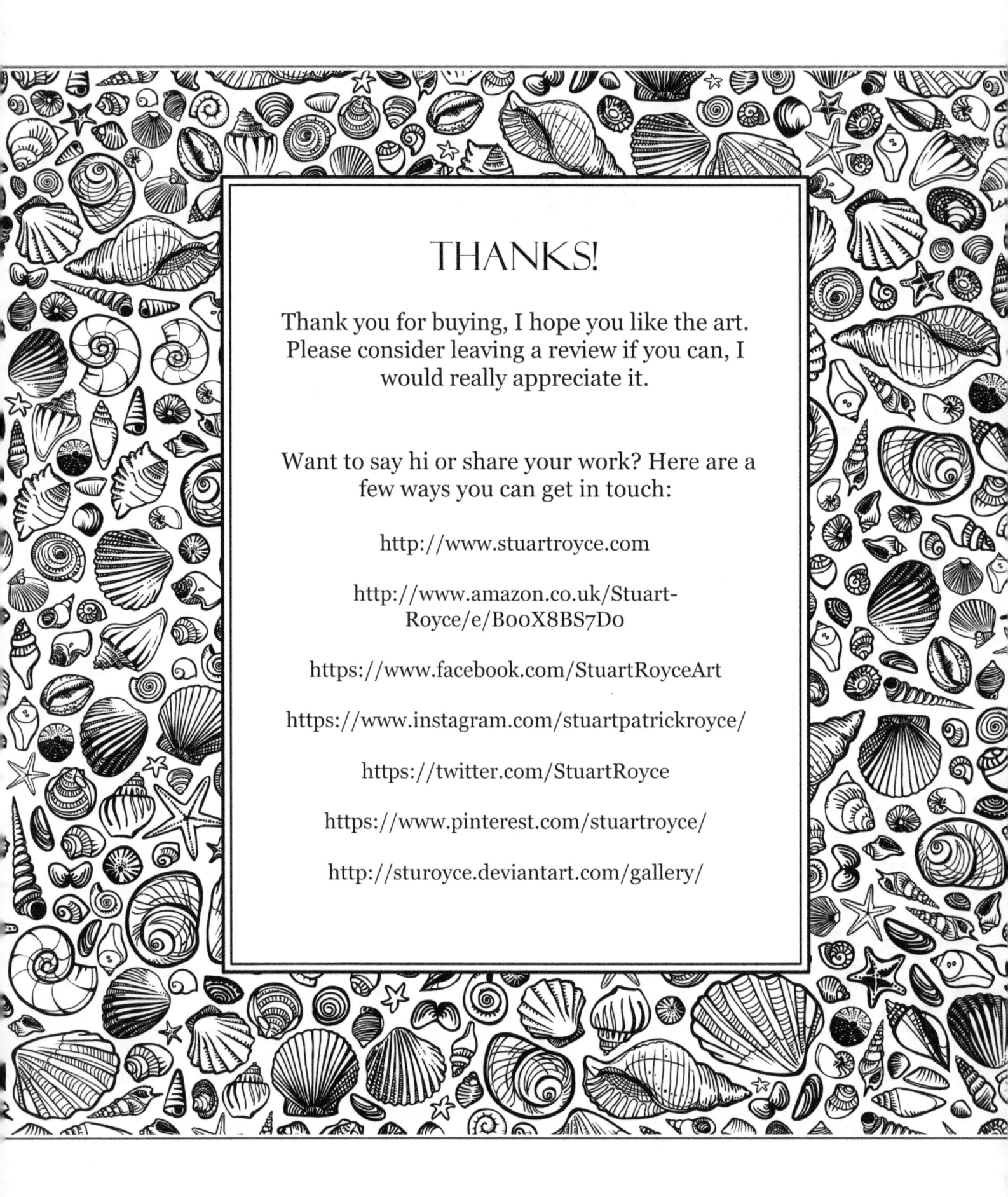

THANKS!

Thank you for buying, I hope you like the art. Please consider leaving a review if you can, I would really appreciate it.

Want to say hi or share your work? Here are a few ways you can get in touch:

http://www.stuartroyce.com

http://www.amazon.co.uk/Stuart-Royce/e/B00X8BS7D0

https://www.facebook.com/StuartRoyceArt

https://www.instagram.com/stuartpatrickroyce/

https://twitter.com/StuartRoyce

https://www.pinterest.com/stuartroyce/

http://sturoyce.deviantart.com/gallery/

OTHERS IN THIS SERIES

Circolour: (Absent-Minded Art Volume 2)

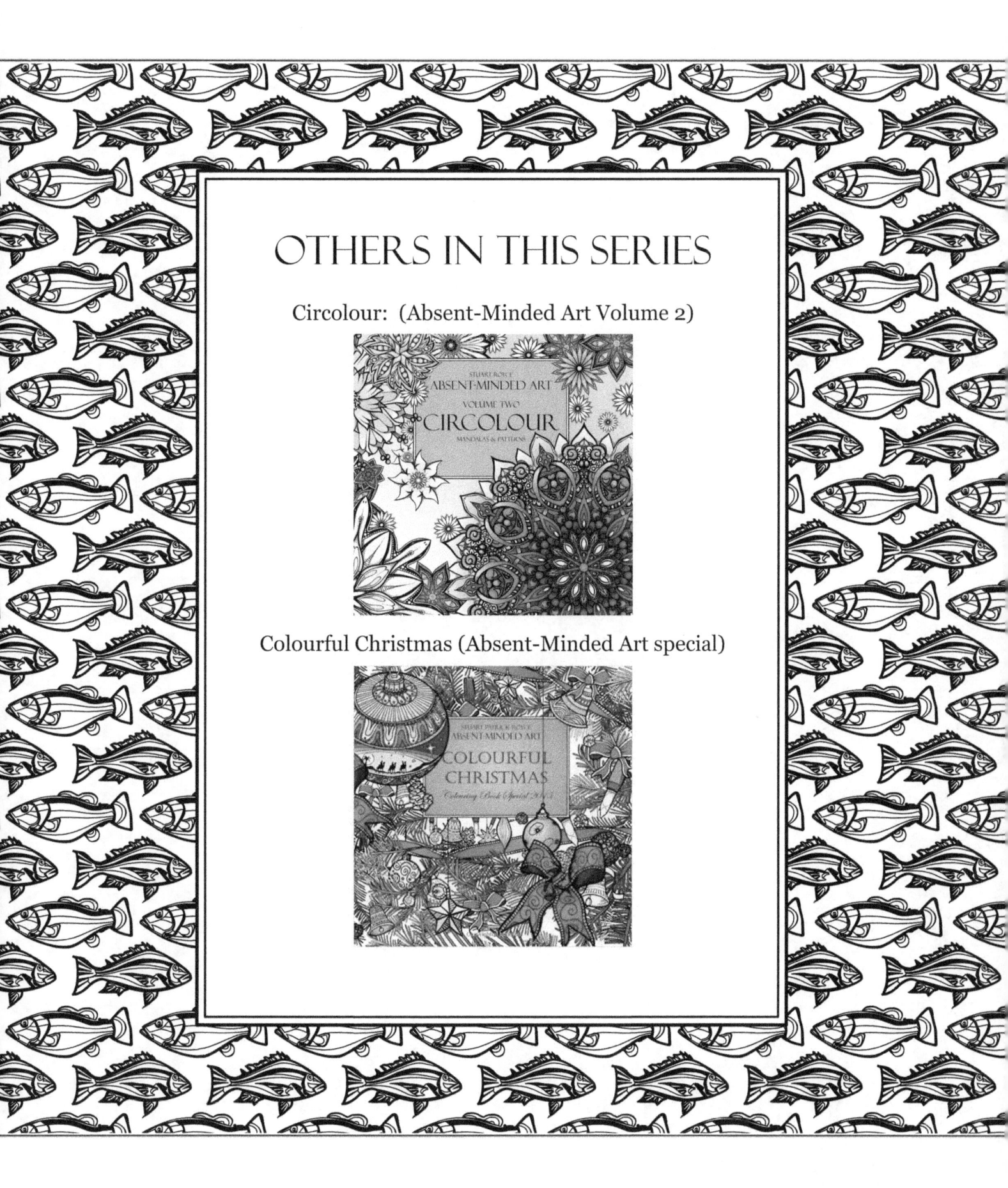

Colourful Christmas (Absent-Minded Art special)

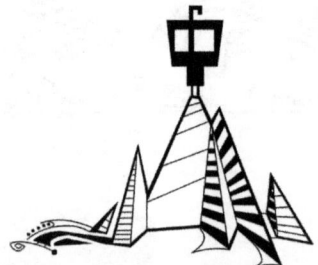

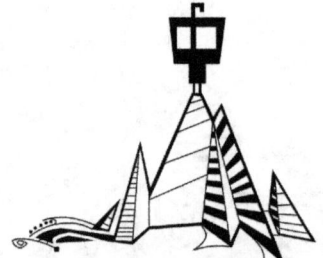

EXTRACT AND USE ME BETWEEN PAGES IF USING INK :)

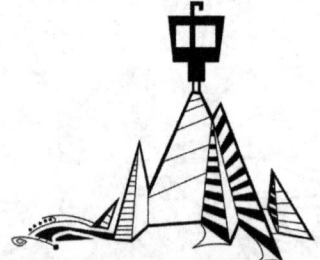